Meredith® Books
Des Moines, Iowa

Meredith Books
1716 Locust Street
Des Moines, Iowa 50309–3023
www.meredithbooks.com

Printed in the United States of America.

First Edition.
Library of Congress Control Number: 2006923867
ISBN-13: 978-0-696-23394-4
ISBN-10: 0-696-23394-0

Food photography by Robert Jacobs
Location photography by Robert Jacobs, Brooke Slezak, Powerhouse Productions

Cover photograph by Brooke Slezak.
Location: The Spotted Dog, Atlanta, Georgia

I dedicate this book to my courageous, proud, and beautiful mother, who always said, "Son, you can do whatever you put your mind to and if you're going to do it, then do it 'til it's done right." I will always love you for the way you made a meal for two feed five; the way you raised five children on your own without a single complaint; how you gave us everything while you had nothing; the way you taught me discipline, strength, character, honesty, and most of all courage—the courage to imagine it, believe it, and now make it real. You are my rock, my role model, my savior. I love you, Mom, and this one is for you.

And to Nola Miles Garvin, my beautiful daughter, my greatest accomplishment, a gift hand-delivered from God: You have forever changed your daddy, as so many said that you would. My only mission in life is to make you proud and see you live, learn, and love. You give my life new purpose, my dearest daughter, my sense of calm, my place of peace, my true north, my precious jewel. —Love, Dad

thanks and acknowledgments

First and foremost, I would like to thank God for all my blessings. Every day I give him praise. I'd also like to thank the following people for their contributions to *Turn Up the Heat* and TV One:

• To Cathy Hughes, Alfred Liggins, Johnathan Rodgers, Karen Wishart, Nikki Webber, Susan Banks, Bernard Bell, Antoinette Leone, Erick Clayton, George Lima, Sitarah Pendelton, Rose-Catherine Pickney, Lee Gaither. Also thanks to Radio One, all the cable providers, and Direct TV for their support.

• To Hugh Walsh, director of photography with an eye like a hawk and the heart of a lion. You're great!

• To Mike Weiss, my friend and attorney: Thank you for helping me hold it all together in a legal way.

• To Cicely Ingram: Thank you for all of your support in The ATL (Atlanta).

• To Laura Corwin, director on the set who calls the shots: Thanks for the times that you've covered me, and with the wave of a hand calmed me down.

• To Shawn (Shizz) Porter, my friend and barber: Thank you for always keeping it Philly crisp!

• To Steven Proudhelm, Brian Postell, B-Sly Williams, and my L.A. Crew: Thank you for your enthusiasm, work ethic, your old-school grind, and of course your encouragement and support.

• To my great business managers Joel Goldstein, Zareh Bandari, Zavik Bandari, and Ashleigh Izzi: Who needs a bank with a crew like you? Thank you.

• To my business partners Tracy and Mitchell Stein: Thank you for the G. Garvin's Restaurant dream you made come true; my introduction to the world on my terms—11/13/01—thank you.

• To Fawn Weaver: 432, respectfully.

• To my *Turn Up the Heat* crew: I am grateful to have a team that works as a family. And a special thanks to Joe, our super-talented editor who does wonders bringing it all together. Nenman, you are the man; your hard work and dedication are greatly appreciated—welcome to the team. Don Lagarde, you are the perfect addition to our crew. As I say on the set, you are my Robert Duvall!

• To D. Maxwell: Yo, D! Thanks for stepping up and making all of this come together.

• To Sitarah Pendelton: Thanks for believing in me from the start. You've been a queen and a friend, and it's not to be forgotten. Thank you so much for making sure the team finishes on top.

• To Nikki Webber: You are a trooper and you're always there for me. Thank you.

• To Traci Lynn: With all of the great things you've done for so many people, you still found time to help one more person (me). Thank you for your trust and friendship.

• To Orlando Jones (The Homie): You're an old friend who started this journey by my side as a southern brother. You have taught me so much about the business of media and the business of life. Blessings, my brother, and I wish you well.

• To my dear friend Sherri McGhee: Thank you for always being honest and for always caring.

• To Remus Andrew Hall and Tobin Montgomery: There is nothing that you do not know about me, and that being said, you're both still my closest friends alive. You have given me the strength to continue when all I had was enough to quit. You have been nothing short of my right and left arms. I love you both and thank you for your great many sacrifices to see me do my thing.

• To my man Andre Ponder, who has always supported the Journey: Thank you.

• To my church family at New Hope AME Baptist Church in Atlanta: A special thank you.

• To Rochelle Brown and Sonia Armstead, two people to whom I owe a great deal: You are not just the producers of TV; you are producers of life. You have taken me, Gerry Garvin, a man with a vision, dream, and goal, and made it real. I imagined it, and you brought it to life. You've helped me to be the G. Garvin that people have grown to know and love. A special place will always be reserved in my heart for the both of you.

• To the team that worked on this book: Jan Miller, Lois White, Erin Burns, Mick Schnepf, Krista Ruane, Francine Matalon-Degni, Robert Jacobs, Brooke Slezak, and Susan Strelecki.

• To my dearest sisters, Renita, Carla, Sheria, and Tonya Garvin: There are no words for the impact that a large family of beautiful, strong black women can bring. I am so lucky and blessed to have you all.

• To my dear grandmothers, Baby Ray Nola Owens and Hattie Garvin: I wish you were here to teach us all the tradition of love, as well as food, truly family style. Rest in Peace! Love, your grandson, Gerry Garvin.

introduction to G

Before we get started, I would like to say thank you for the time that you spend reading this introduction. This being my first book, it may read a little more personal than what you might expect from your typical cookbook. For a person whose life's journey has been supported by so many people, I just felt that telling my story was important. My life has been a series of lessons that I could not have learned alone.

At this point, you might be asking yourself who is Gerry Garvin (AKA G. Garvin) and where did he come from and why should I be interested in his book. My story goes a bit like this: I was born and raised in Atlanta in a single-parent home with four sisters and my mom, all of whom cooked. Though I did know my father, he wasn't around much. The rules were simple. Mom always said, "I will get you all the things you need, but things that you all want, you'll have to get for yourselves." That was our first lesson on responsibility. There were other rules: Come straight home from school, no company. Do your homework. Clean the house (we took turns washing the dishes by the week). Make dinner. Go to church on Sundays. So that's what we did. My sisters and I found at a young age that breaking the rules was not very comfortable on your cushion. That was our first lesson on discipline.

Growing up, a few of the other kids would walk down to the local market to get fresh produce and meats. But back then, our family baked most of our breads, and most of the fish was caught by my uncle Barry or cousins Gene and Louis. This became the only way of life for us, and we loved it. We were poor, happy, and always full.

As I grew older, I was in and out of typical kid trouble, so my mom started to take me to work with her at the Breman Jewish Home. I helped her clean and make food delivery rounds after she and the others prepared meals. She later allowed me to peel potatoes, carrots, and onions; stock and restock the dry storage; wash dishes; and do whatever else to keep me busy. My mom ended up working there for almost 34 years. I literally grew up in the place. Back then, it was simply a way to make extra cash, but in the meantime, I was actually learning my way around the kitchen.

By the time I was 13 years old, I had a part-time job as a dishwasher and prep guy at a local restaurant, The Gathering. This is where I developed my love for food. Only being allowed to work for four hours a day after school, I worked as many days as I could and learned as much as possible. I even worked straight through my summer breaks. The next job came a year later at The Old Vinings Inn where I met my first French chef. Here I learned to use knives and other kitchen equipment in ways I had never known. That was my first lesson in strength and the will to win.

I soon moved on to the Ritz Carlton Hotel in downtown Atlanta. I worked in the gourmet dining room as the grill and vegetable guy, continuing to learn. After two years, I got a promotion and a raise, as well as transfer to a place I had never known—Palm Springs, California. The promotion was the opportunity of a lifetime—in working toward meeting my goal of becoming a chef—but it meant leaving my two greatest loves: my family and my friends. I was completely terrified but I prayed on it, and there I went. The choice was made, and the path was laid. I only had one thing to do, and that was to follow the path.

After two incredibly difficult but gratifying years, I left the Ritz Carlton Hotel and moved to Los Angeles. The place: Noa Noa, where I was sous chef under Ralph Marhinkle. Over the next few years, I traveled the world learning all I could about food. After a short time with the Buckhead Life Group in Atlanta, I settled in Los Angeles for what's turned out to be the next 17 years of my life in the restaurant business. As my career took on a life of its own, I worked as executive chef at Morton's, Kass Bah, and Reign and catered for some of the most powerful people on the planet, with the help of dear friend and event planner, Diane Valentine. And finally at the age of 34, I achieved my goal in opening my own restaurant, G. Garvin's Restaurant, at 8420 W. 3rd St.

After about two years of being open, this incredible woman that I had a crush on in '91 and '92 walked into the restaurant: Traci Lynn. Traci and I became very good friends, and she eventually changed my life. One day I told her about a cooking show idea I had. Then one day she called me to say she had a friend at this new network, TV One, and that she wanted to pitch my show idea.

We met with TV One executive Sitarah Pendelton who believed in me immediately and introduced me to the rest of the TV One family. I knew right away that this was where I was supposed to be. They are the most amazing group of people with vision and passion unlike I have ever seen. I wanted to be a part of this journey, as well as lead as best as I could. TV One welcomed me into their family and put their trust in that same young man from Atlanta who didn't have much but a dream and love for God, family, and food. And for that, I am forever grateful.

Joining TV One has been a wonderful opportunity. Their philosophy of being the destination for lifestyle and entertainment fits right into what I think is important for a television network geared toward presenting the positive side of young African-American lives. The ability to show us in roles of leadership and responsibility with intelligent content is something that has been missing until now. We are making history! Having read a proposal on paper that said my culinary show somehow fit into the network's philosophy might have scared the average TV exec, but TV One believed and allowed me to bring to you the super simple style of *Turn Up the Heat.*

So together we—G. Garvin, TV One, and PowerHouse Productions—now bring you *Turn Up the Heat,* the book. The recipes in this book are full of great memories for me and will give you a sense of who I am. You will find recipes created by me as well as recipes from my incredible mom and grandmom. There are recipes from friends and other family members like my auntie Pat, LaLa, and my cousin Big D. You will also find recipes from my outstanding production team at PowerHouse Productions and my executive sous chef, Dwayne Maxwell. These recipes are full of great memories.

So thank you for your amazing support and love for the network, the show, the book, and—most of all—for me. Without you, I am merely a man with a thought that I often only shared with myself. You have become the recipient of my thoughts, as well as my dreams, delivered to you through my love of food. So please, for me, remember the rules so greatly stated by my friend and barber, Shawn Porter. #1: God first and family, for without whom we are nothing. #2: Exercise your mind and your muscle, as you can only go as far as your mind and body will allow. And #3: Supersize your hustle. You cannot be stopped. Under no circumstance is failure an option. If you can imagine it, then you can make it real. Let no one stand in the way of your future.

"The recipes in this book are full of great memories for me and will give you a sense of who I am."
— Chef G. Garvin

chapter one

super simple

{ Spend a little time in the kitchen to prepare
a flavorful meal that pleases everyone. }

I know that life can sometimes be very complicated. Many times the complications are created by us. You are late for work, can't find parking, or lose your wallet or purse. Maybe the dry cleaner ruined the suit or dress you were going to wear this weekend. When you come home, the house is a mess, and you are exhausted. So why should I ask you to make some insanely difficult meal after a day like that? I love cooking and do it for a living—and even I don't want to take on the challenge of fixing a complex meal after a rough day. So I say let's do things that are simple first and then, like everything else we work on over time, the simple becomes super simple. Life is short. Let's just eat.

chicken saté

makes/12 skewers • see photo, page 102

3   boneless, skinless chicken
    breast halves
1   teaspoon salt
1   teaspoon black pepper
12 6-inch wooden skewers
2   tablespoons olive oil
    Spicy Peanut Sauce
    (see recipe, below)
    Chopped fresh parsley

1. Rinse chicken; trim off excess fat. Season all sides with salt and pepper. Slice chicken lengthwise into 12 strips. Place each chicken strip lengthwise on a skewer.

2. In a sauté pan heat oil over medium-high heat. Place skewers in pan. Sauté for 5 to 6 minutes or until chicken is cooked through, turning skewers to cook evenly.

3. To serve, place chicken skewers on a plate. Drizzle Spicy Peanut Sauce over chicken. Sprinkle with additional pepper and chopped fresh parsley.

G's NOTES

For a clean, polished presentation, wrap the ends of skewers with 3×3-inch squares of foil.

spicy peanut sauce

makes/about 3½ cups • see photo, page 102

¼   cup olive oil
1   cup peanut butter
1   cup heavy cream
¾   cup coconut milk
½   cup chicken stock
3   tablespoons packed
    brown sugar
2   tablespoons chopped shallot
1   tablespoon honey
    Pinch red pepper flakes

1. Heat olive oil in a saucepan. Add peanut butter, cream, coconut milk, chicken stock, brown sugar, shallot, honey, and red pepper flakes. Stir with whisk until smooth and heated through.

quesadillas
makes/6 to 8 servings

2 cups shredded cheddar cheese
2 cups shredded mozzarella
 cheese
1 cup cooked ground beef
1 cup chopped cooked chicken
1 cup chopped cooked shrimp
1 cup sliced red onion
1 cup diced red bell pepper
1 cup diced yellow bell pepper
1 cup guacamole
1 cup sour cream
1 cup salsa
1 package 6-inch flour
 tortillas
 Butter (optional)

1. Set up all ingredients, except tortillas and butter, in separate bowls. Let everyone pick his or her favorite fillings, starting with the cheese, and fill his or her own tortilla. (Don't fill with guacamole, sour cream, or salsa yet.) Fill tortillas and fold in half.

2. To cook on top of the stove, melt 1 teaspoon butter in a large sauté pan over medium heat. Brown quesadillas one at a time in butter, turning to brown on both sides. Repeat for each quesadilla.

3. Serve quesadillas with guacamole, sour cream, or salsa, as desired.

G's NOTES

In most recipes, unsalted butter is always used. However, to add more flavor to the quesadilla, use salted butter.

For a healthier approach, quesadillas can be placed on a baking sheet lined with parchment paper and baked in a 350°F oven for 5 to 10 minutes.

Different types of flavored tortillas are available, like red bell pepper, spinach, Parmesan, and whole wheat. Be creative!

Having kids build their own quesadillas is a great opportunity to get them to help out. The first step is for everyone to wash his or her hands.

catfish bites

makes/4 servings

2 cups canola oil
4 8-ounce pieces catfish fillets, skin removed, cut into bite-size pieces
4 teaspoons seasoned salt
2 teaspoons garlic salt
1½ cups all-purpose flour
Tartar Sauce (see recipe, right)
1 lemon, sliced (optional)

1. In a small, deep sauce pot or a deep-fat fryer heat oil over medium heat.

2. Sprinkle catfish with seasoned salt and garlic salt. Place flour on a plate and dredge catfish pieces in flour. Place catfish strips in hot oil and cook until golden

3. Remove catfish pieces from oil and place on paper towels to absorb excess oil Serve with Tartar Sauce and, if desired, lemon slices.

tartar sauce: In a bowl stir together 1 cup mayonnaise, ¼ cup diced gherkin pickles, 2 tablespoons chopped fresh chives, 2 tablespoons chopped fresh parsley, 2 tablespoons capers, 1 tablespoon chopped shallot, 1 tablespoon Dijon mustard, 1 tablespoon lemon juice, 1½ teaspoons Worcestershire sauce, 1½ teaspoons hot sauce, 1 teaspoon salt, and 1 teaspoon black pepper.

scallops wrapped in **bacon**

makes/6 scallops

6   large scallops
1   teaspoon salt
1   teaspoon coarsely ground
    black pepper
3   strips uncooked bacon
    Olive oil

1. Preheat oven to 350°F. Season scallops with salt and pepper. Cut strips of bacon in half. Wrap a half strip of bacon around each scallop.

2. Line a baking sheet with parchment paper; brush paper lightly with olive oil. Brush wrapped scallops lightly with olive oil and place on baking sheet. Sprinkle scallops with additional pepper.

3. Bake for 10 to 15 minutes or until bacon is cooked and scallops are browned.

quick **potato** salad
makes/4 to 6 servings

6   **medium white potatoes, peeled and sliced**
½   **cup mayonnaise or salad dressing**
¼   **cup chopped onion**
¼   **cup pickle relish**
2   **tablespoons Dijon mustard**
1   **tablespoon chopped garlic**
1   **tablespoon dried Italian seasoning**
1   **teaspoon celery seeds**
1   **teaspoon garlic powder**
1   **teaspoon onion powder**
1   **teaspoon paprika**
⅛   **teaspoon black pepper**
3   **hard-cooked eggs, peeled and diced**

1. Bring a large pot of water to a boil. Add potato slices and boil just until tender but not mushy. Drain; set aside to cool.

2. In a large bowl combine mayonnaise, onion, relish, mustard, garlic, Italian seasoning, celery seeds, garlic powder, onion powder, paprika, and pepper; mix well. Add potato and diced eggs; stir gently to combine. Chill until ready to serve.

shrimp and crab **salad**

makes/4 servings

1   pound large shrimp
4   hard-cooked egg whites, diced
¼   cup mayonnaise or salad
      dressing
¼   cup chopped celery
¼   cup chopped onion
1   tablespoon dried Italian
      seasoning
1½ teaspoons chopped garlic
1   teaspoon onion salt
1   teaspoon Old Bay®
      seasoning
1   teaspoon black pepper
8   ounces lump crabmeat

1. Cook shrimp in shells. When cool, peel, devein, and chop shrimp. Place in a large bowl.

2. To bowl with shrimp, add egg whites, mayonnaise, celery, onion, Italian seasoning, garlic, onion salt, Old Bay seasoning, and pepper; mix together.

3. Drain crabmeat and stir into shrimp mixture. Chill until ready to serve.

𝒢's NOTES
This salad can be served on a bed of lettuce, stuffed in pita bread, or spread on any of your favorite breads.

pasta and broccoli
makes/4 to 6 servings

1	pound spiral pasta (rotini)
1	head broccoli, cut into spears
1	medium onion, sliced
½	cup shredded carrot
¼	cup mayonnaise or salad dressing
1	teaspoon chopped garlic
1	teaspoon seasoned salt
	Black pepper

1. Cook pasta according to package directions; drain.

2. Cook broccoli in small amount of boiling water until tender; drain.

3. In a large bowl combine pasta, broccoli, onion, carrot, mayonnaise, garlic, seasoned salt, and pepper. Mix well.

mozzarella and **tomato salad**
makes/4 servings

8 ounces fresh mozzarella cheese
1 teaspoon salt
1 teaspoon black pepper
3 medium tomatoes
2 tablespoons olive oil
5 fresh basil leaves
   Balsamic Vinaigrette
     (see recipe, below)
   Crushed red pepper (optional)

1. Slice mozzarella cheese into equal rounds; lay them on a serving dish. Season cheese with salt and pepper.

2. Slice tomatoes into equal rounds and layer tomato slices between cheese slices. Drizzle olive oil over all. Top off each tomato and cheese combo with a basil leaf. Drizzle vinaigrette over salad before serving. If desired, sprinkle crushed red pepper over salad to spice it up.

balsamic vinaigrette
makes/about ¾ cup

¼ cup balsamic vinegar
¼ cup olive oil
2 tablespoons Dijon mustard
2 tablespoons packed
     brown sugar
1 teaspoon chopped garlic
1 teaspoon chopped shallot
1 teaspoon black pepper
   Pinch salt

1. In a small bowl combine all ingredients. Whisk until smooth.

parmesan and cheddar cheese grits
makes/6 servings

4   cups water
½   teaspoon salt
1   cup uncooked fine or medium
      hominy grits
½   cup shredded cheddar cheese
¼   cup shredded Parmesan cheese
1   tablespoon unsalted butter
      Black pepper

1. In a small sauce pot bring the water and salt to a boil. Whisk in the grits and continue to whisk for about a minute. When the mixture returns to a boil, reduce heat to low. Cook for 10 to 15 minutes or until creamy and smooth, stirring frequently.

2. Remove pot from heat. Stir in cheeses, butter, and pepper to taste.

black-eyed pea soup

makes/6 to 8 servings • see photo, page 97

3 tablespoons olive oil
½ cup chopped white onion
½ cup chopped celery
¼ cup chopped shallot
4 cloves garlic, crushed
    and chopped
1 pound andouille sausage
½ cup (1 stick) unsalted butter
1 teaspoon red pepper flakes
    Salt and black pepper
2 15-ounce cans black-eyed peas
4 cups chicken stock
1 cup heavy cream
1 tablespoon hot sauce
    Fried Leek (see recipe, below)
1 bunch fresh cilantro, chopped

1. Heat 2 tablespoons of the olive oil in a large pot over medium heat. Stir in onion, celery, shallot, and garlic. While this cooks for a minute or two, dice the uncooked sausage. Add half of the sausage to the pot.

2. In a sauté pan heat the remaining 1 tablespoon olive oil over medium heat. Brown the remaining sausage. Once brown, use a paper towel to soak up excess oil in pan; set sausage aside.

3. Add butter, red pepper flakes, and salt and black pepper to taste to the onion mixture in the pot. Let cook for 3 to 4 minutes. Add black-eyed peas to pot; cook for a couple of minutes. Add chicken stock. Bring to a simmer; reduce heat to low. Cook for 15 minutes. Stir in cream and hot sauce.

4. To serve, ladle soup into a bowl and top with Fried Leek, browned sausage, and cilantro.

fried leek

makes/4 to 6 servings

1 leek*
1 teaspoon salt
1 teaspoon black pepper
½ cup cornstarch
    Canola oil

1. Cut off green part of leek and peel off the first layer of leaves. Rinse well. Cut leek in half lengthwise; place flat side down and cut into very thin strips. Place leek strips in a bowl of cold water (enough to float leek) and move strips around in water to release any sand. Place leek in a strainer; shake off excess water.

2. Season drained leek strips with salt and pepper. Place cornstarch in a bowl. Add leek and coat well with cornstarch. Place leek in a fryer** of hot oil until golden brown. Use a slotted spoon to remove leek from fryer; place on paper towels to absorb excess oil. Use fried leek as a garnish for desired dish.

* Sliced onion may be substituted for leek.
** Using a fryer is suggested. To fry in a frying pan, add 1 inch of canola oil to pan and heat to frying temperature (use a frying thermometer as a guide).

G's NOTES

When preparing leeks, slicing them first and floating them in water lets any sand fall to the bottom of the bowl or sink. For extra-dirty leeks, this step may be repeated.

split pea soup with **pancetta**

makes/6 to 8 servings

½ cup olive oil
8 ounces pancetta (Italian bacon), diced small
1 tablespoon chopped garlic
1 tablespoon chopped shallot
1 medium onion, diced small
3 stalks celery, diced small
2 carrots, diced small
1 16-ounce bag dried split peas, sorted and rinsed*
2 quarts chicken stock
1 tablespoon chopped fresh thyme
1 tablespoon salt
1½ teaspoons black pepper
4 to 6 ounces fresh spinach

1. In a stockpot heat olive oil over medium heat. Add pancetta and cook out all the fat. Add garlic and shallot; sauté until tender. Add onion, celery, and carrot; sauté until tender.

2. Stir in split peas; combine well. Add chicken stock, thyme, salt, and pepper. Bring to a boil. Reduce heat and simmer until peas are soft and are falling apart (add more stock if necessary). Remove from heat and cool slightly.

3. Place a few ladles of soup into a blender and add a couple handfuls of spinach. Blend until spinach is incorporated. Place soup in a second pot. Repeat with remaining soup and spinach. Warm soup over very low heat.

* Sort through split peas and remove any stones or shriveled peas. Rinse under cold water and drain.

G's NOTES
Fresh spinach gives the soup a bright clean color.

candied yams

makes/6 servings

3   large yams
2   cups water
½   cup packed brown sugar
½   cup granulated sugar
½   cup (1 stick) butter
1   tablespoon ground cinnamon
1   teaspoon vanilla
¼   teaspoon ground nutmeg
½   cup crushed pecans (optional)

1. Peel and cut yams into ½-inch rounds. In a medium pot combine yams and remaining ingredients except pecans. Simmer over medium heat until yams are tender and sauce is sticky and coats the yams. If desired, sprinkle with pecans.

chicken pot pie
makes/4 servings • see photo, page 98

¼ cup olive oil
½ cup chopped celery
½ cup chopped carrot
2 tablespoons chopped garlic
2 tablespoons chopped shallot
½ cup chopped asparagus
  (blanched*)
½ cup chopped onion
½ cup corn
½ cup snow peas
¼ teaspoon salt
¼ teaspoon black pepper
5 cups chicken stock
½ cup + 1 tablespoon heavy cream
⅓ cup sweetened condensed milk
6 cooked chicken breast
  halves, diced
⅓ cup cornstarch
¼ cup water
6 tablespoons unsalted butter
2 tablespoons chopped fresh
  rosemary and thyme
2 sheets frozen puff pastry, thawed
1 egg

1. Preheat oven to 350°F. In a large saucepan heat olive oil over medium-high heat. Add celery, carrot, garlic, and shallot to pan; sauté for 2 minutes. Add asparagus, onion, corn, and snow peas. Season with salt and pepper. Pour in chicken stock, ½ cup cream, and sweetened condensed milk. Add chicken and bring to a simmer.

2. In a small bowl stir together cornstarch and the water to create a thickening agent, then pour into pot; stir until thickened and bubbly. Stir in butter until melted. Stir in rosemary and thyme; remove from heat.

3. Cut puff pastry sheets in half, then set aside. Beat egg and the 1 tablespoon cream together; set aside.

4. Fill four individual ceramic baking dishes evenly with chicken mixture. Cover each dish with a piece of puff pastry. Pinch edges to seal and cut off excess around sides. Take a fork and poke a few holes in top of puff pastry. Brush puff pastry with egg mixture.

5. Bake pot pies about 35 minutes or until crust is golden brown.

* To blanch asparagus, plunge it in boiling water for a minute or two until its color turns bright green. Place it immediately in ice water; drain well.

chicken with a **spicy chili** sauce

makes/4 servings

1 pound boneless, skinless
    chicken breast
1 yellow bell pepper
1 red bell pepper
1 medium zucchini
1 medium yellow squash
1 bunch enoki mushrooms
8 ounces Chinese long beans
2 tablespoons peanut oil
2 tablespoons chicken stock
2 tablespoons chili garlic sauce
    Hot cooked white rice

1. Rinse chicken; pat dry with paper towels. Thinly slice chicken; set aside. Cut peppers into strips; set aside. Cut zucchini and yellow squash in half lengthwise, then cut at an angle into half moons; set aside. Trim mushrooms; set aside.

2. Trim long beans into 5-inch pieces. Bring a pot of water to a boil. Add beans to water and blanch for 30 seconds. Remove from boiling water and place in a bowl of ice water. Drain beans and pat dry.

3. Heat a wok over medium-high heat; add peanut oil. When oil begins to smoke, add chicken and stir continuously until almost done. Add all vegetables, stirring frequently, until heated through.

4. Add chicken stock and chili sauce; combine thoroughly. Serve over rice.

 's NOTES

String beans may be substituted for Chinese long beans. These specialty beans may be found at your local Asian market.

vegetable **fried rice**
makes/4 servings

3	tablespoons peanut oil
¼	head Chinese cabbage, chopped
4	scallions, chopped
2	tablespoons chopped garlic
1	teaspoon chopped fresh ginger
½	cup green peas
½	cup julienned or shredded carrot
3	eggs, beaten
2	cups steamed white rice
2	tablespoons soy sauce
	Salt
	Black pepper
1	tablespoon chopped fresh parsley

1. Have all vegetables ready to go. Heat a wok over medium-high heat; add peanut oil. When oil begins to smoke, add cabbage, scallions, garlic, and ginger; stir well. Add peas and carrot; mix well.

2. Push vegetables to the side of the wok, making a hole in the center. Add eggs to hole and scramble, mixing cooked eggs into vegetables. Add rice and combine well. Stir in soy sauce and season to taste with salt and pepper. Sprinkle with parsley and serve hot.

curry chicken

makes/4 to 6 servings

1	whole chicken, cut up
	Salt
	Black pepper
3	tablespoons olive oil
1	cup sliced carrot
½	cup chopped shallot
3	cloves garlic, chopped
3	tablespoons curry powder
4	potatoes, peeled and sliced
2	large onions, sliced
2	cups chicken stock

1. Wash pieces of chicken; pat dry. Season chicken with salt and pepper; set aside.

2. Heat olive oil in a large pot over medium heat. Add ½ cup of the carrot, the shallot, and garlic. Place pieces of chicken into pot; stir. Add curry powder, then half of the potato and onion. Sprinkle with additional salt and pepper; stir. Stir in chicken stock. Add remaining ½ cup carrot, potato, and onion.

3. Bring to a boil; reduce heat. Cover and simmer for 35 to 40 minutes or until chicken is no longer pink and vegetables are tender.

G's NOTES

This recipe can also be made with thighs. Or ask your butcher to cut the chicken to your liking or use your favorite pieces. Whatever you decide, be sure to use fresh chicken.

apple brandy chicken
makes/4 servings

½ cup olive oil
4 6-ounce boneless, skinless
   chicken breast halves
   Salt
   Black pepper
1 cup all-purpose flour
2 tablespoons unsalted butter
1 tablespoon chopped shallot
2 Red Delicious apples,
   peeled, cored,
   and sliced
½ cup apple juice
¼ cup brandy
½ cup heavy cream

1. In a large sauté pan heat olive oil over medium heat. Season chicken with salt and pepper. Dredge chicken in flour. Add chicken to pan and sauté until golden brown.

2. Add butter and shallot; sauté until tender. Add apple slices; sauté until tender. Add apple juice; simmer for 2 to 3 minutes. Add brandy; simmer for 3 more minutes. Add cream; simmer until sauce is thickened.

G's NOTES
This dish can be served over rice, mashed potatoes, or grilled vegetables.

chicken paillard with angel hair pasta

makes/4 servings

½ cup olive oil
1 tablespoon salt
  Black pepper
1 16-ounce box angel hair pasta
4 6-ounce boneless, skinless
    chicken breast halves
½ cup all-purpose flour
1½ cups white wine
1 lemon, juiced
2 tablespoons chopped garlic
2 tablespoons chopped shallot
1 tablespoon small capers
½ cup heavy cream
2 tablespoons unsalted butter
1 tablespoon chopped fresh
    Italian parsley

1. Bring a large pot of water to a boil. Add 2 tablespoons of the olive oil, the salt, and a pinch of pepper. Add pasta and cook for 3 to 5 minutes or until desired tenderness. Strain pasta and toss with 2 tablespoons of the olive oil. Set aside and keep warm.

2. Place chicken between two pieces of plastic wrap and lightly pound until slightly flat. Sprinkle chicken with salt and pepper. Dredge both sides of chicken in flour.

3. Heat the remaining ¼ cup olive oil in a large sauté pan over medium heat. Sauté chicken until no longer pink. While chicken is sautéing, add wine, lemon juice, garlic, shallot, and capers to pan.

4. Place pasta on a plate. When mixture comes to light simmer, remove chicken and lay on top of pasta. Add cream and butter to remaining juices in pan. Stir until butter is melted. Stir in the parsley and additional salt and pepper to taste. Pour mixture over chicken and pasta.

G's NOTES

If you like, you can remove the chicken from the skillet and toss the pasta in the finished sauce before serving.

andouille **succotash stew**

makes/4 to 6 servings

1	tablespoon olive oil
1	pound andouille sausage, diced
2	tablespoons chopped shallot
1	tablespoon chopped garlic
2	tablespoons tomato paste
12	ounces canned baby lima beans
2	cups whole kernel corn
1	teaspoon salt
	Pinch black pepper
	Pinch cayenne pepper
3	cups chicken stock
2	cups diced plum tomato
¼	cup water
1	tablespoon cornstarch

1. In a sauté pan heat olive oil over medium heat. Add sausage, shallot, and garlic; cook for 3 to 5 minutes or until shallot and garlic are soft. Add tomato paste; mix well. Stir in lima beans, corn, salt, black pepper, and cayenne pepper. Cook for 2 minutes, stirring frequently.

2. Add chicken stock. Bring to a boil; reduce heat. Simmer for 20 to 25 minutes or until lima beans are tender. Add tomato; cook for 5 minutes more. In a small bowl combine water and cornstarch until smooth. Stir into stew; cook and stir until thickened.

smothered **pork chops**
makes/6 servings

1	cup canola oil
6	4-ounce pork chops, thinly cut
	Salt
	Black pepper
1½	cups all-purpose flour
2	tablespoons unsalted butter
1	large onion, sliced
1	cup water
	Drop Biscuits (see recipe, below)

1. Preheat oven to 350°F. In a large ovenproof frying pan heat canola oil over medium heat. Season pork chops with salt and pepper, then dredge in 1 cup of the flour. Shake off excess flour. Add pork chops to pan and brown on both sides. Remove pork chops and set aside.

2. Add butter to pan; let melt. Add onion and cook until almost brown. Stir in the remaining ½ cup flour and continue to cook until the desired color is reached. (See G's Notes.) Add water and whisk until smooth. Season with additional salt and pepper.

3. Return pork chops to pan. Cover and bake for 25 minutes. To serve, crumble biscuits on plates and top with pork chops and gravy.

 G's NOTES
For dark gravy, cook flour for longer time over low heat.
For light gravy, cook flour for less time over higher heat.

drop biscuits
makes/12 biscuits

3	cups all-purpose flour
4	teaspoons baking powder
1	tablespoon sugar
1	teaspoon salt
1	teaspoon baking soda
¼	cup unsalted butter
1¼	cups buttermilk
2	eggs, lightly beaten
1	teaspoon canola oil

1. Preheat oven to 375°F. In a large bowl stir together the flour, baking powder, sugar, salt, and baking soda. Using a large fork, cut the butter into the flour mixture until well incorporated.

2. In a separate bowl mix the buttermilk and eggs together. Add all but 2 tablespoons of the buttermilk mixture to the flour mixture; stir until moistened. (Dough should be moist and sticky.)

3. Grease a baking sheet with the canola oil. Drop spoonfuls of dough onto prepared baking sheet about 1 inch apart. Brush the tops with the remaining buttermilk mixture.

4. Bake for 10 to 15 minutes or until biscuits are golden brown and spring back when lightly touched or a toothpick inserted in the middles comes out dry.

tacos
makes/10 tacos

1 **package taco shells**
2 **cups shredded lettuce**
1 **cup cooked ground beef with taco seasoning added**
1 **cup cooked peeled shrimp**
1 **cup shredded cooked chicken**
1 **cup shredded cheddar cheese**
1 **cup diced tomato**
1 **cup sour cream**
1 **cup guacamole**
1 **cup mild salsa**

1. Bake 10 taco shells in a 375°F oven for 5 minutes. Set up remaining ingredients in separate bowls. Let everyone fill his or her own taco shells.

 's NOTES

This is a great recipe for kids to get involved in making their own. Taco seasoning can be found in the grocery store to add to the meat for flavor. Also, if using shrimp, season it with seasoned salt.

beef **stir-fry** with plum sauce

makes/4 servings

1   pound beef flank steak
2   tablespoons peanut oil
2   tablespoons chopped garlic
1½ cups julienned or
    shredded carrot
1   bunch scallions, cut into
    1-inch slices
1   small green bell pepper,
    diced small
1   small yellow bell pepper,
    diced small
1   small orange bell pepper,
    diced small
½   cup bamboo shoots
¼   cup soy sauce
¼   cup chicken stock
3   tablespoons dark plum sauce
    Hot cooked white rice

1. Cut steak lengthwise and then against the grain, making thin strips. Have all the vegetables ready to go.

2. Heat a wok over medium-high heat; add peanut oil. When oil begins to smoke, add garlic, then beef, moving meat continuously. Add carrot, scallion, bell pepper, and bamboo shoots, stirring frequently until heated through. Add soy sauce, chicken stock, and plum sauce; combine thoroughly. Serve over rice.

roast beef sandwiches
makes/4 servings

2   6-inch hero rolls
¼   cup unsalted butter, softened
2   tablespoons chopped garlic
    Salt
    Black pepper
4   tablespoons Dijon mustard
    Goat Cheese Spread
      (see recipe, below)
1   red onion, sliced in rings
¼   cup olive oil
8   ounces sliced cooked roast beef
1   roasted red bell pepper,
      cut into strips
8   slices Swiss cheese

1. Cut rolls in half horizontally. Spread softened butter on cut sides of bread. Sprinkle chopped garlic on buttered sides of bread; use a spatula to pat garlic into bread. Sprinkle with salt and pepper to taste. Place rolls on ungreased baking sheet. Lightly toast under broiler 4 to 5 inches from heat for 2 to 4 minutes. (Watch carefully so bread does not burn.)

2. Remove rolls from oven. Spread mustard on toasted rolls. Spread Goat Cheese Spread over mustard. Add a few rings of onion to bottom halves of rolls. Top with a drizzle of olive oil and a pinch of black pepper.

3. Add the roast beef, roasted pepper strips, and Swiss cheese. Top with the remaining olive oil and another pinch of black pepper. Close sandwiches; cut in half.

G's NOTES

This delicious sandwich can also be served on sourdough rolls, French baguette, or focaccia bread.

goat cheese spread
makes/about 1 cup

8   ounces goat cheese (chèvre)
3   tablespoons olive oil
1   teaspoon chopped garlic
1   teaspoon chopped shallot
1   teaspoon chopped fresh
      parsley
1   teaspoon salt
    Black pepper

1. Place goat cheese in a bowl. With a fork or rubber spatula, mash and break apart goat cheese. Add remaining ingredients and mix until smooth.

G's NOTES

Olive oil makes the spread smooth. This is a mayonnaise replacement. You can store this delicious goat cheese spread for up to 3 days in your refrigerator.

lamb stew
makes/6 to 8 servings

¼ cup olive oil
2 pounds boneless leg of
   lamb, cubed
1½ teaspoons seasoned salt
2 tablespoons chopped garlic
2 tablespoons chopped shallot
1 tablespoon tomato paste
6 cups chicken stock
½ cup red wine
1 teaspoon chopped fresh
   thyme
1 teaspoon chopped fresh
   rosemary
1 bay leaf
   Salt
   Black pepper
3 medium Yukon gold potatoes,
   peeled and diced
2 parsnips, diced
2 carrots, diced
2 leeks, diced
1 small celery root, diced

1. In a stew pot heat olive oil over medium heat. Sprinkle lamb with seasoned salt. Add lamb to pot and brown well on all sides. Add garlic and shallot; cook for 2 to 3 minutes. Stir in tomato paste until well combined. Add chicken stock, wine, thyme, rosemary, and bay leaf. Season with salt and pepper.

2. Reduce heat. Cover and simmer about 30 minutes or until meat is tender. Add potato, parsnip, carrot, leek, and celery root. Simmer about 15 minutes more or until vegetables are tender. Adjust seasonings, if necessary. Before serving, remove bay leaf.

shrimp with **black bean sauce** and asian vegetables

makes/4 servings

2 pounds U-15* shrimp
¼ cup peanut oil
¾ cup sliced carrot
¾ cup sliced celery
2 small onions, sliced
2 cups sliced baby bok choy
1 large red bell pepper, sliced
1 cup snow peas
20 ears baby corn
¼ cup chicken stock
3 to 4 tablespoons black
   bean garlic sauce
   Hot cooked white rice
¼ cup chopped scallion

1. Peel and devein shrimp; set aside. Have all vegetables ready to go.

2. Heat a wok over medium-high heat; add peanut oil. When oil begins to smoke, add shrimp and stir continuously until shrimp just start to turn pink. Add carrot, celery, and onion; stir. Add bok choy, bell pepper, snow peas, and baby corn, stirring frequently until heated through.

3. Add chicken stock and black bean sauce; combine thoroughly. Serve over rice. Garnish with chopped scallion.

* U-15 means under 15 shrimp per pound. They are also called jumbo shrimp.

 's NOTES

The ingredients for my Asian recipes can generally be found in your local supermarket. However, the baby bok choy may not be readily available, so regular bok choy may be substituted.

sautéed **salmon**
makes/4 servings

4 8-ounce pieces salmon fillet
2 teaspoons salt
2 teaspoons black pepper
¼ cup olive oil
   Tomato and Basil Sauce (see
      recipe, below)
   Fried Leek (see recipe, page 22)

1. Season salmon with salt and pepper on one side. Pat seasonings into fish.

2. In a large sauté pan heat olive oil over medium heat. Add salmon, seasoned sides down. Cook until browned, then flip over to brown other sides. Remove from pan and place on paper towels to absorb excess oil.

3. To serve, spoon Tomato and Basil Sauce onto center of serving dish. Place salmon on top of sauce, then top with Fried Leek.

G's NOTES
Here is a twist on sautéed salmon. Leave the skin on the salmon and scale it. Cut slits into the skin about 1 to 2 inches long. In a nonstick pan sauté fish skin side down first. Once skin is crispy, carefully turn it over and cook to desired doneness.

tomato and **basil sauce**
makes/4 servings

¼ cup olive oil
4 cups diced fresh plum tomato
1 15-ounce can diced tomatoes,
      drained
2 tablespoons chopped garlic
2 teaspoons chopped shallot
1 cup white wine
¼ teaspoon cracked black pepper
6 fresh basil leaves, finely chopped
   Salt

1. In a sauté pan heat olive oil over medium heat. Remove pan from heat and add all tomato, garlic, and shallot. Return pan to heat. Add wine and pepper to pan. Stir the mixture and let simmer until sauce is slightly thickened. Stir in basil and salt to taste. Keep warm over low heat until ready to serve.

rigatoni primavera with garlic and butter sauce
makes/4 servings

5 tablespoons olive oil
2 teaspoons salt
2 teaspoons black pepper
1 zucchini
1 yellow squash
1 small head broccoli
1 pound rigatoni
2 tablespoons chopped garlic
1 tablespoon chopped shallot
1 red bell pepper, seeded
   and sliced
1 cup halved cherry tomatoes
1 small onion, sliced
1 cup vegetable stock
2 tablespoons unsalted butter
3 tablespoons grated Parmesan
   cheese
1 tablespoon chopped
   fresh parsley

1. Fill a large pot with water; add 2 tablespoons of the olive oil, 1½ teaspoons of the salt, and 1 teaspoon of the black pepper. Bring to a boil.

2. Cut zucchini and yellow squash in half lengthwise and scrape out the seeds with a spoon. Cut halves into ¼-inch half moons. Cut the broccoli into florets. Place zucchini, squash, and broccoli in a hand strainer and submerge them in the boiling water for 30 seconds. Remove and place in a bowl of ice water for 1 minute. Drain and set aside.

3. Place rigatoni in boiling water. Boil for 10 minutes or until tender; drain.

4. Meanwhile, in a large sauté pan heat the remaining 3 tablespoons olive oil over medium heat. Add garlic and shallot; cooking until slightly browned. Add bell pepper, tomato, onion, zucchini, yellow squash, and broccoli. Stir vegetables to cook evenly.

5. Add vegetable stock and the remaining 1 teaspoon black pepper and ½ teaspoon salt. Bring to a boil and simmer for 3 minutes. Finish sauce by whisking in butter until melted; stir in Parmesan cheese and parsley. Serve over rigatoni.

chapter two
family style

{ Create memories around your table with some of G. Garvin's best-loved dishes. }

The reason I like to serve my dishes family style is that it gives the meal memory. We can all eat at any time and at any place we want—but what is the point if you're just eating to satisfy your hunger? To shop, prepare, and serve a meal with friends and family just means so much more. It is a time to share the intimate details of our lives, and there is nothing more important than that. Make no mistake, if you are single and living alone, a great meal just for yourself can sometimes be a treat, especially if you need alone time. But trust, there is always a hungry neighbor who can join you. Start with a recipe that has been in your family for a while—or try an idea in this chapter. Whatever you do, trust these words: Family means one thing—for all our shortcomings, love won't yield.

g's fresh lemonade
makes/about 2 quarts

2   quarts water
8   lemons, juiced
1   cup sugar
1   pint whole strawberries
1   bunch mint leaves
    Ice
1   lemon, sliced

1. In a pitcher combine water and lemon juice. Add sugar and stir until dissolved. Add whole strawberries and mint leaves. Pour into glasses filled with ice and garnish with lemon slices.

corn bread
makes/8 to 10 servings

1   cup yellow cornmeal
¾   cup all-purpose flour
¾   cup sugar
2   tablespoons baking powder
2   teaspoons salt
¾   cup milk
2   large eggs, beaten
½   cup canola oil
1   tablespoon sour cream
1   tablespoon unsalted butter

1. Preheat oven to 350°F. In a bowl combine cornmeal, flour, sugar, baking powder, and salt. Make a well in the center of the dry ingredients. Add milk, eggs, and canola oil; mix all together. Fold in sour cream.

2. Grease a loaf pan with the butter. Pour batter into prepared pan. Bake for 25 to 30 minutes or until golden brown and a toothpick inserted into the center comes out clean.

corn bread **dressing**
makes/10 to 12 servings

1   batch corn bread*
½   cup (1 stick) butter
2   medium onions, diced
4   stalks celery, diced
1½   teaspoons poultry seasoning
1½   teaspoons dried sage leaves
2   cups chicken stock
½   cup heavy cream

1. First, prepare corn bread; set aside. Preheat oven to 350°F. In a large saucepan melt butter over medium heat. Add onion and celery; sauté until tender. Stir in poultry seasoning and sage. Crumble in corn bread and combine well. Stir in chicken stock and cream; mix well.

2. Pour corn bread mixture into a greased 13×9×2-inch pan. Bake for 30 to 35 minutes or until golden.

* Use my recipe for Corn Bread (above) or a boxed mix.

corn bread **mashed potatoes**

makes/8 to 10 servings • see photo, page 99

1	batch corn bread*
5	Idaho potatoes
	Pinch salt
½	cup milk
¼	cup butter
¼	cup heavy cream
½	teaspoon salt
½	teaspoon black pepper
1	teaspoon chopped fresh parsley

1. First, prepare corn bread; set aside. Next, wash and peel the potatoes; cut them into small cubes. Place the potato cubes in a pot of cold water with a pinch of salt. Boil for 15 to 20 minutes or until tender.

2. When the cubes are fully cooked, strain them from the hot water and return them to the hot pan. Add the milk, butter, and cream. Mash cubes until you have the texture you want (lumpy or smooth).

3. Cut a large piece of corn bread and crumble it into mashed potato mixture. Add salt, pepper, and parsley; mix well. Garnish each serving with a small slice of corn bread.

* Use my recipe for Corn Bread (opposite) or a boxed mix.

corn bread, bacon, and **blue cheese** mashed potatoes

makes/8 to 10 servings

1	batch corn bread*
10	Idaho potatoes
	Pinch salt
2	cups heavy cream
1	cup (2 sticks) unsalted butter
1	cup blue cheese crumbles
8	ounces bacon, chopped and fried crisp
5	scallions, chopped
1	tablespoon minced garlic (optional)

1. First, prepare corn bread; set aside. Next, wash and peel the potatoes; cut them into small cubes. Place the cubes in a pot of cold water with a pinch of salt. Boil for 15 to 20 minutes or until tender.

2. When the potato cubes are fully cooked, strain them from the hot water and return them to the hot pan. Add the cream, butter, blue cheese, bacon, scallion, and, if desired, garlic. Mash until you have the texture you want (lumpy or smooth). Crumble in the corn bread and mix well.

* Use my recipe for Corn Bread (above opposite) or a boxed mix.

garlic broccoli
makes/6 to 8 servings

Pinch salt
2 heads broccoli, cut into florets
1 tablespoon olive oil
2 tablespoons chopped garlic
2 tablespoons chopped shallot
2 tablespoons unsalted butter
Salt
Black pepper

1. Place 2 quarts of water in a pot with a pinch of salt; bring to a boil. Add broccoli and blanch for 5 to 8 minutes. Remove broccoli from water and place in ice water until cool. Drain and pat dry.

2. In a sauté pan heat olive oil over medium heat. Add garlic and shallot to pan. Add broccoli and sauté until desired doneness. Stir in butter. Season to taste with salt and pepper.

string beans
makes/4 to 6 servings

1 tablespoon salt
1 pound string beans, trimmed and cut into 2-inch lengths
2 tablespoons olive oil
1 medium onion, diced small
1 clove garlic, chopped
Seasoned salt
Black pepper

1. Place 1 cup of water in a pot with 1 tablespoon salt; bring to a boil. Add beans and cook for 20 minutes. Drain.

2. In a large nonstick skillet heat olive oil over medium heat. Add onion and garlic; cook about 3 minutes or until soft. Add the string beans; cover skillet. Cook beans just until tender, stirring occasionally. Season to taste with seasoned salt and pepper.

holiday cabbage
makes/8 to 10 servings

1 medium head green cabbage (about 2½ pounds)
¼ cup unsalted butter
1 medium onion, diced small
2 medium carrots, cut into ½-inch dice
½ cup diced red bell pepper
¼ cup diced organic rainbow carrot (optional)
2 large russet or Idaho potatoes, peeled and cut into 1-inch cubes
2 cups chicken stock
2 tablespoons chopped garlic
2 tablespoons chopped shallot
1 tablespoon salt
1 tablespoon red pepper flakes
1 tablespoon chopped fresh cilantro (optional)
1 tablespoon chopped fresh parsley (optional)

1. Cut cabbage into quarters. Cut off and discard hard core from each quarter. Slice cabbage into ½-inch-wide strips; set aside.

2. In a large skillet melt butter over medium heat. Add the onion, carrot, bell pepper, and, if desired, rainbow carrot. Cook about 5 minutes or until soft, stirring often. Stir in cabbage and potato. Stir in chicken stock, garlic, shallot, salt, and red pepper flakes.

3. Bring to a boil; reduce heat to medium-low. Cover and simmer about 20 minutes or until potato is tender and most of the liquid is gone. Transfer cabbage mixture to a serving dish and, if desired, sprinkle with the cilantro and/or parsley.

three-cheese au gratin potatoes

makes/6 to 8 servings

- 3 tablespoons unsalted butter
- 5 large potatoes, peeled, cooked, and sliced
- 2 tablespoons chopped garlic
- 2 tablespoons chopped shallot
- 2 teaspoons salt
- 1 teaspoon black pepper
- 1 teaspoon paprika
- 1 cup shredded cheddar cheese
- 1 cup shredded Swiss cheese
- 1 cup shredded smoked cheddar cheese
- 1 cup heavy cream
- 1 cup milk

1. Preheat oven to 375°F. Coat a 13×9×2-inch baking dish with the butter. Arrange one-third of the potato in dish. Sprinkle with one-third of the garlic, shallot, salt, pepper, and paprika. Sprinkle one-third of the cheeses over potato. Repeat layers two more times. Pour cream and milk over all.

2. Cover and bake for 25 minutes. Uncover and bake for 5 to 10 minutes more or until bubbly and potato is lightly browned.

five-cheese macaroni and cheese

makes/8 to 10 servings

1   2-pound package elbow
    macaroni
½   cup (1 stick) unsalted butter
8   medium eggs
1   cup milk
1   14-ounce can sweetened
    condensed milk
2   cups shredded mozzarella
    cheese
1   cup shredded sharp
    cheddar cheese
1   cup shredded mild
    cheddar cheese
¾   cup shredded Parmesan cheese
¾   cup crumbled feta cheese
1   tablespoon seasoned salt
1   teaspoon salt
1   teaspoon black pepper

1. Preheat oven to 325°F. Bring a large pot of water to boil; add macaroni. Cook according to package directions until tender; drain. Place cooked macaroni in a large bowl. Add the butter, stirring until melted; set aside.

2. In a separate bowl place eggs, milk, and sweetened condensed milk; beat with a whisk until smooth. Pour mixture over macaroni and stir gently to coat.

3. In another bowl combine all the cheeses. Set aside about one-fourth of the cheese mixture. Add remaining cheese mixture, the seasoned salt, salt, and pepper to macaroni mixture. Fold together with a rubber scraper. If mixture is too stiff, add more milk.

4. Sprinkle a little of the reserved cheese mixture over the bottom of a 3-quart casserole dish. Spoon macaroni and cheese mixture into dish; smooth over top with rubber scraper. Sprinkle remaining cheese mixture on top. Bake, uncovered, about 30 minutes or until golden and bubbly.

rice bake

1	pound boneless, skinless chicken breast, sliced
2	teaspoons salt
2	teaspoons black pepper
¼	cup + 3 tablespoons olive oil
1	pound spicy Italian sausage links
1	cup chopped onion
½	cup (1 stick) unsalted butter
¼	cup all-purpose flour
2	cups milk
2	tablespoons Worcestershire sauce
1	teaspoon cayenne pepper
1	teaspoon dry mustard
1	teaspoon seasoned salt
1	cup shredded mozzarella cheese
1¼	cups shredded cheddar cheese
¼	cup water
2	cups cooked rice
¼	cup bread crumbs

1. Preheat oven to 350°F. Season sliced chicken breasts with 1 teaspoon of the salt and 1 teaspoon of the black pepper. In a sauté pan heat ¼ cup of the olive oil over medium-high heat. Add chicken pieces; cook until halfway cooked, then add Italian sausages.

2. When chicken is cooked completely, remove it from pan and place on paper towels to absorb excess oil. When sausages are browned on both sides, place them on paper towels as well. When sausages cool, slice them into ½-inch rounds and set aside.

3. In the same sauté pan heat the remaining 3 tablespoons olive oil over medium-high heat. Add onion and sauté for 1 to 2 minutes or until slightly browned. Add half of the butter, the remaining 1 teaspoon salt, and the remaining 1 teaspoon black pepper. When the butter is melted, stir in the flour.

4. Return chicken and sausage to pan; mix well. Stir in milk, Worcestershire sauce, cayenne pepper, dry mustard, and seasoned salt. Stir in mozzarella cheese and 1 cup of the cheddar cheese. Let cheese melt, then reduce heat. Stir in water to loosen mixture. Remove from heat and set aside.

5. Coat a medium casserole dish with the remaining ¼ cup butter. Spread 1 cup of the cooked rice over bottom of dish. Spread half of the meat and cheese mixture over rice. Repeat layers. Sprinkle the remaining ¼ cup cheddar cheese and the bread crumbs over top. Bake, uncovered, for 25 to 30 minutes or until golden brown and heated through.

chicken **stew**

makes/4 servings

1 large onion
3 medium tomatoes, cored
1 16-ounce can peeled plum
    tomatoes, drained
    (reserve liquid)
½ Scotch bonnet pepper, seeded
    (see tip, page 207)
1½ teaspoons chopped fresh ginger
4 cloves garlic
½ cup olive oil
2 pounds chicken (legs or thighs
    may be used), skin and
    fat removed
3 cups chicken stock
1 teaspoon dried thyme
1 teaspoon celery salt
1 teaspoon ground allspice
2 bay leaves

1. Chop half of the onion; set aside. Place remaining half onion in a food processor or blender with the cored tomatoes, canned tomatoes, Scotch bonnet pepper, ginger, and garlic. Process or blend until smooth, adding reserved liquid from canned tomatoes as needed to make a smooth purée.

2. In a large pot cook chopped onion in oil over medium-high heat until it is slightly brown. Add the tomato purée to pot. Cook for 12 to 15 minutes or until liquid is reduced and sauce is not acidic tasting.

3. Add chicken, chicken stock, thyme, celery salt, allspice, and bay leaves to pot. Bring to boiling; reduce heat. Simmer for 20 to 25 minutes more or until chicken is no longer pink, stirring occasionally. Before serving, remove bay leaves.

G's NOTES

If you wish to add bouillon cubes instead of using chicken stock, just combine 3 cubes with enough water to equal 3 cups.

fried chicken

makes/4 to 6 servings • see photo, page 100

1	whole chicken, quartered
3	cups canola oil
2	cups all-purpose flour
1½	tablespoons seasoned salt
1½	tablespoons garlic salt
1	tablespoon paprika
1½	teaspoons black pepper
½	teaspoon salt

1. Wash pieces of chicken and place in a bowl of ice water. In a deep frying pan heat canola oil over medium-high heat.

2. Pour flour into a bowl. Season flour with 1 tablespoon of the seasoned salt, 1 tablespoon of the garlic salt, and the paprika; mix well. Remove chicken from ice bath and set on plate. Sprinkle chicken with the remaining seasoned salt and garlic salt, the pepper, and the ½ teaspoon salt. Coat all sides of chicken pieces with seasoned flour. Pat off excess flour.

3. Place each piece of chicken in hot oil. Fry about 15 minutes, turning pieces occasionally until cooked thoroughly and golden brown. Remove chicken from pan. Place on plate lined with paper towels to soak up excess oil.

G's NOTES

Placing chicken in an ice bath helps the flour to coat the chicken better. For the ice bath, use equal parts of ice and water.

collard greens with smoked turkey bacon
makes/6 to 8 servings • see photo, page 104

¼ cup olive oil
8 ounces smoked turkey
   bacon, chopped
1 large onion, sliced
3 small shallots, chopped
4   to 6 cloves garlic, chopped
2 pounds collard greens
2 cups chicken stock
1 cup water
½ cup white wine
   Salt
   Black pepper

1. In a large sauté pan heat olive oil over medium heat. Add bacon. Then add onion, shallot, and garlic. Reduce heat to low and cook until bacon is crispy, stirring occasionally.

2. Meanwhile, separate and thoroughly rinse collard green leaves under water. Roll 2 to 3 leaves together; slice roll crosswise into thin strips. Add collard greens to pan; stir to combine.

3. Pour in chicken stock, water, and wine. (Add more water, if needed, to cover greens.) Cover pan, increase heat to medium, and simmer for 30 minutes or until desired tenderness, stirring occasionally. Season to taste with salt and pepper.

braised chicken
with plum tomatoes and potatoes
makes/4 to 6 servings

2 tablespoons olive oil
2 pounds chicken thighs
3 teaspoons seasoned salt
   Kosher salt
   Black pepper
4 medium Yukon gold potatoes,
   peeled and quartered
2 medium onions, diced small
2 tablespoons unsalted butter
6 cloves garlic, smashed
2 tablespoons chopped shallot
1 cup white wine
1 cup chicken stock
1 8-ounce can whole,
   peeled plum
   tomatoes, crushed
2 sprigs fresh thyme, chopped

1. Preheat oven to 375°F. In a large roasting pan heat olive oil over medium heat on stovetop.

2. Wash chicken and pat dry with paper towels. Season with 1 teaspoon of the seasoned salt and the kosher salt and pepper. Season potato with the remaining 2 teaspoons seasoned salt. Place chicken and potato in hot roasting pan and brown on all sides.

3. Add onion, butter, garlic, and shallot to pan. Add white wine, chicken stock, undrained tomato, and thyme to pan. Cover pan with foil and place in the oven for 25 minutes or until chicken is no longer pink.

G's NOTES
You can use your favorite chicken parts for this recipe.

bow tie pasta and **chicken**
makes/4 to 6 servings

4	tablespoons olive oil
	Salt
1	16-ounce package bow tie pasta
1	pound boneless, skinless chicken breasts, cooked
8	asparagus spears (blanched*)
2	tablespoons chopped garlic
2	tablespoons chopped shallot
1	cup chopped tomato
½	cup tomato sauce
¼	cup grated Parmesan cheese
2	tablespoons chopped fresh basil
2	teaspoons chopped fresh Italian parsley
½	teaspoon black pepper
3	tablespoons unsalted butter
	Grated Parmesan cheese
	Chopped fresh basil and fresh Italian parsley

1. In a large pot combine 2 quarts of water with 2 tablespoons of the olive oil and a pinch salt; bring to a boil. Add pasta; cook according to package directions until tender. Drain pasta; place in a bowl and keep warm.

2. Break chicken into small pieces and set aside. Chop asparagus into 1-inch pieces and set aside.

3. In a medium pot heat the remaining 2 tablespoons olive oil over medium high heat. Add chicken, asparagus, garlic, and shallot; stir. Add chopped tomato, tomato sauce, the ¼ cup Parmesan cheese, 2 tablespoons basil, 2 teaspoons parsley, the pepper, and a pinch of salt; stir. Reduce heat to low and let simmer for 10 minutes.

4. Add pasta to pot and stir to combine. Add butter and stir until melted. Spoon mixture onto serving platter. Garnish with additional Parmesan cheese, basil, and parsley.

* To blanch asparagus, place it in boiling water for a minute or so until it turns bright green. Transfer asparagus to ice water. Drain well.

G's NOTES
Grate your own Parmigiano-Reggiano, pecorino, or ricotta salata cheese. This gives your pasta a better taste than with pregrated cheese. Also, never rinse pasta after cooking; you wash all the vitamins down the drain.

penne rigate with **chicken and asaparagus** in pink sauce

makes/4 servings

¼   cup + 2 tablespoons olive oil
1   tablespoon + 2 teaspoons
      kosher salt
8   ounces penne rigate
1   tablespoon + 1 teaspoon
      black pepper
1   pound asparagus
4   plum tomatoes
½   roasted chicken
2   tablespoons chopped shallot
1   tablespoon chopped garlic
5   fresh basil leaves
½   cup white wine
½   cup heavy cream
2   tablespoons tomato paste
2   tablespoons unsalted butter
3   tablespoons grated
      Parmesan cheese

1. Fill a 6-quart stockpot with water and bring to a boil. Also fill a 3-quart pot with water and bring to a boil over medium heat.

2. To the 6-quart pot add ¼ cup of the olive oil and 1 teaspoon of the salt. Add the penne rigate and boil for 4 to 6 minutes or until al dente (firm to the tooth). Drain pasta and set aside.

3. To the 3-quart pot add 1 tablespoon of the salt and 1 tablespoon of the pepper. Drop asparagus into the boiling water and cook for 4 minutes. Transfer asparagus to a bowl of ice water. Drain, then place on paper towels to absorb excess water. Cut into 1-inch pieces; set aside.

4. Place plum tomatoes into the same pot of boiling water for 1 to 2 minutes to loosen skins. Transfer tomatoes to the ice water for 1 minute. Peel the skin off of the tomatoes and dice tomatoes; set aside.

5. Remove bones and skin from chicken and break meat apart. In a large skillet heat the remaining 2 tablespoons olive oil over medium heat. Add the chicken, shallot, and garlic; sauté for 2 minutes. Stir in diced tomato, the basil, the remaining 1 teaspoon salt, and 1 teaspoon pepper.

6. Add wine, cream, tomato paste, and butter; mix until butter is melted. Add the cooked pasta; toss to coat. Add asparagus and Parmesan cheese; toss to combine. Place mixture in a large pasta bowl and garnish with additional Parmesan cheese.

rigatoni **filetto**
makes/4 to 6 servings

Pinch salt
10 whole plum tomatoes
8 whole cloves garlic
¼ cup olive oil
8 ounces pancetta or bacon,
   cut into thin strips
2 Italian sausage links,
   skin removed
1 large onion, diced small
2 tablespoons chopped shallot
½ cup white wine
2 tablespoons chopped fresh basil
   Salt
   Black pepper
1 16-ounce box rigatoni
1 tablespoon unsalted butter
   Grated Parmesan cheese

1. Preheat oven to 375°F. In a large pot bring 2 quarts of water with a pinch of salt to a boil.

2. Core tomatoes and place them in a roasting pan with garlic cloves. Coat tomatoes and garlic with the olive oil. Roast tomatoes and garlic until garlic is golden brown, rotating them in the pan occasionally to cook evenly. Remove from oven and set aside to cool.

3. Remove the tomatoes and garlic from pan and chop; set aside. Pour the oil from roasting pan into a large saucepan and heat over medium heat. Add pancetta; cook for 5 minutes. Add sausage to pan and continue cooking until pancetta turns brown. Add onion and shallot; cook until soft. Add chopped tomato and garlic, white wine, and basil; mix well. Simmer for 10 to 15 minutes. Season to taste with salt and pepper.

4. While sauce simmers, add rigatoni to boiling water and cook until desired doneness. To finish the sauce, stir in butter until melted. Drain pasta and add to sauce; mix well. Top each serving with Parmesan cheese.

citrus-glazed ham
makes/10 to 12 servings

2   cups chicken stock
1   cup pineapple juice
1   cup orange juice
½   cup packed brown sugar
3   tablespoons honey
1   teaspoon ground cinnamon
1   4- to 5-pound smoked ham
10 to 15 whole cloves

1. Preheat oven to 375°F. For glaze, in a small saucepan stir together chicken stock, pineapple juice, orange juice, brown sugar, honey, and cinnamon. Bring to a boil, stirring to dissolve brown sugar. Remove from heat.

2. Place ham on a rack in a roasting pan. Spike ham with cloves; pour glaze over ham. Roast ham for 1 hour or until internal temperature is 155°F, basting every 15 minutes.

short ribs of beef

makes/4 servings

¼   cup olive oil
4   8-ounce boneless beef short ribs
½   teaspoon salt
½   teaspoon black pepper
½   teaspoon seasoned salt
½   teaspoon garlic salt
1   cup all-purpose flour
1   white onion, diced small
2   carrots, peeled and diced small
2   stalks celery, diced small
1   cup red wine
2   cups chicken stock
2   cups veal stock or beef stock
2   cups water
1   14.5-ounce can diced
      tomatoes
2   tablespoons
      Worcestershire sauce
6   medium red potatoes,
      diced small

1. Preheat oven to 300°F. In a large ovenproof sauté pan heat olive oil over medium-high heat.

2. Season short ribs on all sides with salt, pepper, seasoned salt, and garlic salt. Pat seasonings into meat. Dredge short ribs in flour; pat off excess flour.

3. Place short ribs in sauté pan and sear until browned on both sides. Add onion, carrot, and celery; sauté for 3 minutes. Add wine and simmer for 5 minutes. Stir in chicken stock, veal stock, water, undrained tomatoes, and Worcestershire sauce. Bring to a simmer.

4. Cover and place in oven. Roast for 2½ hours or until meat falls from bones. During the final 30 minutes, add potato and cover again.

G's NOTES

Be sure to check the liquid in the pan occasionally to make sure there is enough to keep the meat moist and simmering. Add more stock if necessary.

pot roast
makes/10 to 12 servings

3   tablespoons olive oil
1   4-pound trimmed beef brisket
     Salt
     Black pepper
10   small red potatoes
2   cups sliced shallot
4   carrots, peeled and cut into
        2-inch pieces
4   cups beef stock
1   cup red wine
1   tablespoon chopped
        fresh parsley
4   cloves garlic, peeled and halved
1   teaspoon seasoned salt
1   teaspoon chopped fresh thyme
1   cup sliced button mushrooms

1. Preheat oven to 350°F. In a 5-quart Dutch oven or large roasting pan heat olive oil over medium heat. Season the brisket with salt and pepper. Add brisket to Dutch oven and brown on all sides. Add potatoes, shallot, and carrot; cook for 10 minutes or until vegetables are lightly browned.

2. Add beef stock, red wine, parsley, garlic, seasoned salt, and thyme. Bring to a boil. Cover with a tight-fitting lid. Place in the oven for 2½ hours or until beef is very tender. Add mushrooms to Dutch oven in the last ½ hour. Slice beef and serve with roasted vegetables.

oxtails

makes/4 to 6 servings • see photo, page 101

3   pounds oxtails, sliced
    ½ inch thick
1½ teaspoons salt
1⅛ teaspoons black pepper
1   teaspoon seasoned salt
½   teaspoon + ⅛ teaspoon
    garlic salt
1   cup all-purpose flour
¼   cup + 3 tablespoons canola oil
8   whole canned plum tomatoes
½   cup chopped carrot
½   cup chopped celery
½   cup chopped fresh plum
    tomato
½   cup chopped onion
6   cups chicken stock
2   cups chopped, peeled potato

1. Preheat oven to 300°F. Rinse oxtails. Season oxtails on both sides with 1 teaspoon of the salt, 1 teaspoon of the pepper, the seasoned salt, and ½ teaspoon of the garlic salt. Pat seasonings into meat to seal in flavor. Dredge oxtails in flour; pat off excess flour.

2. Heat ¼ cup of the canola oil in sauté pan over medium high heat. Sear oxtails on both sides in hot pan. Add whole tomatoes to pan; set aside.

3. In a separate sauté pan heat the remaining 3 tablespoons canola oil over medium heat. Add carrot, celery, chopped tomato, and onion. Season vegetables with the remaining ½ teaspoon salt, ⅛ teaspoon garlic salt, and ⅛ teaspoon pepper. Reduce heat to low and let cook down for 10 to 15 minutes.

4. Transfer oxtails and whole tomatoes to a large casserole dish. Pour carrot mixture into dish. Add chicken stock. Cover and place in oven. Roast for 3 hours or until meat is falling off bone. In the last 30 minutes, add potato and cover again.

G's NOTES

It's OK to add the potato during the last 30 minutes of cooking time.

62

southern fried steak with gravy
makes/3 servings • serve with rainbow green beans

¼ cup olive oil
3 6-ounce pieces sirloin steak,
   pounded thin
1 tablespoon seasoned salt
1 tablespoon black pepper
1 cup + 2 tablespoons
   all-purpose flour
2 tablespoons unsalted butter
1 large onion, sliced
1 green bell pepper, diced
2 tablespoons chopped shallot
1 tablespoon chopped garlic
½ cup chicken stock
½ cup beef stock
½ cup heavy cream

1. In a large skillet heat olive oil over medium-high heat. Season steak on both sides with seasoned salt and black pepper. Place the 1 cup flour on a plate. Dredge steak in the flour. Place steak in skillet and brown for 2 minutes per side. Remove steak to a serving platter; set aside and keep warm.

2. In the same skillet melt 4 teaspoons of the butter. Stir in onion, bell pepper, shallot, and garlic; sauté for 2 minutes. Stir in 2 tablespoons flour; mix well. Add chicken and beef stock. Simmer until gravy thickens. Slowly stir in cream. To finish gravy, stir in the remaining butter until melted. Spoon gravy over steak. Serve with Rainbow Green Beans (see recipe, opposite).

rainbow green beans
makes/4 to 6 servings • serve with southern fried steak with gravy

1   pound green beans
2   tablespoons olive oil
3   tablespoons chopped garlic
3   tablespoons chopped shallot
½   cup shredded carrot
½   cup chopped yellow and
      red bell pepper
2   tablespoons unsalted butter
1   teaspoon salt
1   teaspoon black pepper

1. Bring a pot of water to a boil. Add green beans and boil for 5 minutes. Remove beans from pot and place in a bowl of ice water. Drain well.

2. In a skillet heat olive oil over medium-high heat. Add garlic and shallot; sauté for 5 minutes. Add the carrot and toss to combine. Stir in green beans and the bell pepper. Finish by stirring in butter until melted. Season with salt and black pepper.

g's **meatballs** and spaghetti
makes/4 to 6 servings • see photo, page 105

8	ounces ground beef
8	ounces ground veal
4	tablespoons + 2 teaspoons olive oil
1	medium egg
2	teaspoons bread crumbs
2	teaspoons chopped fresh basil
1	teaspoon chopped garlic
1	teaspoon chopped shallot
½	teaspoon salt
½	teaspoon black pepper
	G's Spaghetti Sauce (see recipe, opposite)
	Pinch salt
1	16-ounce box spaghetti

1. Preheat oven to 350°F. Place the ground beef and ground veal in a large bowl. Add 2 teaspoons of the olive oil, the egg, bread crumbs, basil, garlic, shallot, salt, and pepper; mix well. Roll meat mixture into desired-size balls.

2. In a sauté pan heat 2 tablespoons of the olive oil over medium-high heat. Sauté meatballs in pan about 5 minutes or until brown. Remove meatballs from pan and place in a shallow baking pan. Bake for 5 to 7 minutes more or until firm and cooked through. Place meatballs on paper towels to absorb excess oil. Place meatballs in sauce and heat through.

3. Bring a large pot of water with the remaining 2 tablespoons olive oil and a pinch of salt to a boil. Add spaghetti and boil for 7 to 10 minutes or just until tender; drain. Top spaghetti with meatballs and sauce.

g's spaghetti sauce
makes/4 to 6 servings • see photo, page 105

¼ cup olive oil
8 cloves crushed garlic
1 teaspoon chopped shallot
½ cup ground beef
½ cup ground veal
1 teaspoon salt
½ teaspoon black pepper
1 16-ounce can peeled
    whole plum tomatoes
2 cups diced plum tomato
½ cup diced green bell pepper
½ cup diced red bell pepper
2 tablespoons tomato paste
2 whole garlic cloves
4 cups water
2 tablespoons unsalted butter
2 tablespoons grated Parmesan
    cheese
2 teaspoons chopped fresh basil
2 teaspoons chopped
    fresh oregano
1 teaspoon chopped fresh thyme

1. In a large pot heat olive oil over medium-high heat. Add chopped garlic and shallot; stir and let brown. Add beef and veal and let brown. Season with ½ teaspoon of the salt and the black pepper. Gently crush canned tomatoes by hand; add to pot. Add the diced tomato, green and red bell peppers, tomato paste, and garlic cloves; stir.

2. Use a hand-held blender to chop whole tomatoes and blend sauce in pot; stir sauce. Stir in water, butter, and the remaining ½ teaspoon salt. Stir in Parmesan cheese, basil, oregano, and thyme. Let sauce cook down until desired texture.

curried lamb

makes/8 servings

2 pounds boneless leg of lamb
2 limes, juiced
5 scallions, chopped
2½ tablespoons curry powder
4 cloves garlic, chopped
¼ Scotch bonnet pepper, seeded and diced (see tip, page 207)
1 tablespoon chopped fresh thyme
2 teaspoons chopped fresh basil
1 teaspoon grated fresh ginger
1 teaspoon salt
1 teaspoon black pepper
Pinch ground allspice
½ cup olive oil
2 large onions, diced small
3½ cups chicken stock
2 tablespoons unsalted butter
2 tablespoons coconut cream

1. Cut lamb into small pieces; place in a bowl. Add the lime juice, scallion, curry powder, garlic, Scotch bonnet pepper, thyme, basil, ginger, salt, black pepper, and allspice; mix well. If desired, marinate lamb for 1 hour.

2. In a stew pot heat olive oil over medium heat. Remove lamb from marinade; reserve marinade. Brown lamb and onion in hot oil. Add reserved marinade and the chicken stock to pot. Bring to a boil; reduce heat. Simmer, uncovered, about 30 minutes or until lamb is tender. Stir in butter and coconut cream; cook for 10 minutes more. Serve with Coconut Rice and Beans and Fried Plantains (see recipes, opposite).

coconut rice and beans
makes/6 servings

2	tablespoons olive oil
2	scallions, sliced
1	tablespoon chopped garlic
1	tablespoon chopped shallot
1½	cups white rice
2½	cups chicken stock
½	cup coconut milk
2	sprigs fresh thyme
1½	teaspoons seasoned salt
2	cups canned red kidney beans*
2	tablespoons butter
	Salt
	Black pepper

1. Heat olive oil in a medium pot over medium heat. Add scallion, garlic, and shallot; sauté for 2 to 3 minutes or until soft. Add rice and stir to coat. Add chicken stock and coconut milk; bring to a boil. Stir in thyme and seasoned salt. Reduce heat.

2. Cover and simmer about 15 minutes or until rice is nearly tender. Add beans and butter. Return to a simmer. Continue cooking for 5 to 10 minutes or until rice is tender and liquid is absorbed. Before serving, remove thyme sprigs, stir rice, and adjust flavor with salt and pepper.

* If you wish to use dried beans, soak them overnight and cook to your liking.

fried plantains
makes/6 servings

3	ripe yellow plantains
2	cups vegetable oil

1. Peel and slice plantains at an angle. Heat oil in a deep skillet or cast iron skillet. (Oil should be about 3 inches deep.) Brown plantain slices in oil evenly on both sides, turning plantains frequently. Remove and place fried plantains on a plate lined with paper towels to absorb excess oil.

lemon-pepper salmon
makes/4 servings • serve with oven-stewed tomatoes

3 tablespoons olive oil
4 8-ounce pieces salmon
   fillet, skinless
1 tablespoon lemon-pepper
   seasoning
   Salt
   Black pepper
1 tablespoon chopped garlic
1 tablespoon chopped shallot
1 tablespoon unsalted butter
2 lemons, halved
⅓ cup water

1. Preheat oven to 350°F. In a sauté pan heat 2 tablespoons of the olive oil over medium heat. Season salmon with the lemon-pepper seasoning and salt and pepper. Sauté salmon in pan for 3 minutes or until golden brown. Turn salmon over and cook for 2 minutes more. Add garlic, shallot, and butter to pan.

2. Place the salmon and pan drippings in a baking dish. Squeeze the lemons over salmon; add the water, the remaining 1 tablespoon olive oil, and a pinch pepper. Bake for 5 to 7 minutes or until fish flakes easily. Serve with Oven-Stewed Tomatoes (see recipe, below).

oven-stewed tomatoes
makes/4 servings • serve with lemon-pepper salmon

5 plum tomatoes, halved
   lengthwise
1 teaspoon salt
1 tablespoon black pepper
1 tablespoon olive oil
2 tablespoons chopped garlic
2 tablespoons chopped shallot
1 tablespoon chopped
   fresh parsley
½ cup chicken stock
½ cup white wine

1. Preheat oven to 350°F. Season tomato halves with salt and pepper. Place tomato halves, cut sides up, in a lightly greased baking pan. Set aside.

2. In a sauté pan heat olive oil over medium heat. Add garlic, shallot, and parsley; sauté until soft. Spoon garlic mixture evenly on top of tomatoes. Add chicken stock and white wine to pan. Bake, uncovered, for 30 to 45 minutes.

flash-fried tilapia
makes/4 servings

¾ cup canola oil
6 4-ounce pieces fresh tilapia
  Seasoned salt
  Black pepper
¾ cup all-purpose flour

1. In a sauté pan heat canola oil over medium-high heat.

2. Season tilapia on both sides with seasoned salt and pepper. Dredge fish in flour. Fry fish quickly in very hot oil until golden brown. Serve with Fried Corn (see recipe, below).

fried corn
makes/6 to 8 servings

10 ears corn, peeled and cleaned
½ cup canola oil
8 strips bacon, diced
1 onion, diced
1 tablespoon chopped shallot
1 tablespoon chopped garlic
¼ cup all-purpose flour
1 cup chicken stock
  Salt
  Black pepper

1. Cut kernels off of the ears of corn, scrape out juices, and set aside.

2. Heat canola oil in a sauté pan over medium-high heat. Add diced bacon and cook until bacon is crispy. Add onion, shallot, and garlic; reduce heat.

3. Add corn, mix well, and cook for 5 minutes. Add flour and combine well; cook for an additional 3 to 5 minutes. Add chicken stock; simmer for 10 to 15 minutes, stirring frequently. Season to taste with salt and pepper.

g's **fried catfish**
makes/4 servings

2   eggs
½   cup heavy cream
1   cup all-purpose flour
1   cup cornmeal
4   6-ounce catfish fillets
2   teaspoons kosher salt
2   teaspoons black pepper
2   to 4 ounces mixed greens
     Basil Mayonnaise (see recipe,
        page 230)

1. For catfish, place the eggs and cream into a bowl and whisk until combined; set aside. Place the flour on a large plate; set aside. Place cornmeal on a separate plate. Season catfish on both sides with salt and pepper.

2. In a large frying pan heat the remaining ½ cup olive oil over medium heat. Dredge fish in the flour. Next dip fish into the egg and cream mixture, then dredge fish in the cornmeal. Gently place fish into hot oil and cook for 3 minutes per side or until golden brown. Place fried fish on paper towels to absorb excess oil.

3. To serve, place fish on a serving plate and scoop Basil Mayonnaise onto the side of the plate. Garnish with mixed greens and drizzle with additional olive oil.

seafood bouillabaisse

makes/6 to 8 servings • see photo, page 106

8	ounces king crab legs
1	lobster tail
8	ounces sea bass
8	ounces salmon
4	ounces halibut
¼	cup olive oil
9	black mussels, cleaned
8	clams
2	tablespoons chopped garlic
2	tablespoons chopped shallot
2	teaspoons salt
2	teaspoons black pepper
6	ounces calamari, cut into rings
12	medium shrimp, peeled and deveined
4	diver scallops
6	potatoes, peeled and sliced
6	plum tomatoes, peeled and crushed
½	cup sliced cherry tomatoes
2	cups Lobster Stock (see recipe, right)
2	cups water
1	cup white wine
6	fresh basil leaves

1. Chop crab legs between joints and use a kitchen shears to cut along the lighter-colored underside of the shell. Remove crabmeat from legs. Remove shell from lobster meat. Chop crab and lobster meat into 1-inch pieces; set aside. Chop sea bass, salmon, and halibut into 2-inch chunks; set aside.

2. In a large sauté pan heat olive oil over medium heat. Add mussels and clams; cook until they start to open. Add garlic, shallot, salt, and pepper. Sauté for 45 seconds. Add crab, lobster, sea bass, salmon, and halibut to pan.

3. Add calamari, shrimp, and scallops. Stir in potato, crushed tomato, and cherry tomatoes. Add Lobster Stock, water, wine, and basil. Bring to a simmer; reduce heat to low. Cover and cook for 15 minutes.

4. Stir stew with a large spoon. Let sit for 5 minutes before serving. Serve with toasted bread or your favorite rice.

lobster stock: In a large stockpot heat ¼ cup olive oil over medium-high heat. Add 3 pounds raw lobster shells* and sauté until pink. Add 2 tablespoons tomato paste; 1 large onion, rough chopped; 4 shallots, chopped; 6 cloves garlic, crushed; 2 bay leaves; 1 tablespoon black peppercorns; and 2 sprigs fresh thyme. Cook for 5 minutes. Add 1 head celery, rough chopped, and 3 medium carrots, rough chopped. Then add enough water to cover shells, about 4 cups. Bring to a boil; reduce heat. Simmer, uncovered, for 45 minutes. Remove from heat. Strain shells, seasonings, and vegetables from stock and discard. Makes about 4 cups.

* You may use lobster tail or claw shells.

gumbo
makes/10 to 12 servings

Gumbo Stock (see recipe, opposite)
Roux (see recipe, right)
1   pound chicken drumettes (disjointed wing drumsticks)
¼ cup olive oil
2   3-ounce andouille sausage links, sliced
2   3-ounce lamb sausage links, sliced
2   3-ounce Italian sausage links, sliced
2   pounds large shrimp, peeled and deveined
1   pound crawfish tails, peeled
1   pound fresh okra, sliced
2   large leeks, cleaned and diced
2   tablespoons hot sauce
1   teaspoon salt
1   teaspoon black pepper
1   pound lump crabmeat
1   pound back fin crabmeat
1   tablespoon gumbo filé powder
    Hot cooked rice

1. Preheat oven to 350°F. Place Gumbo Stock in a large pot and stir in Roux. Bring to a simmer.

2. Place chicken drumettes on a baking sheet. Bake for 10 to 15 minutes or until cooked through.

3. In a large saucepan heat olive oil over medium heat. Add sausage, shrimp, crawfish tails, okra, and leek. Sauté until all meat and seafood is cooked well. Add to Gumbo Stock with drumettes; cook for 10 minutes or until stock boils. Add hot sauce, salt, and pepper. Add crabmeat and filé powder; simmer for 5 minutes. Serve Gumbo over rice.

roux: In a saucepan melt ½ cup (1 stick) unsalted butter over medium heat. Gradually stir in ½ cup all-purpose flour. Reduce heat to medium-low. Cook for 5 minutes, stirring constantly, until Roux turns light brown.

gumbo stock

makes/about 6 cups

¼ cup olive oil
2 pounds shrimp shells
1 white onion, rough chopped
3 celery stalks, rough chopped
2 carrots, peeled and rough
    chopped
2 scallions, chopped
1 garlic bulb, halved
1½ teaspoons whole
    peppercorns
2 fresh bay leaves
1 teaspoon salt
1 teaspoon black pepper
2 cups white wine
4 cups water
1 bouquet garni

1. In a large pot heat olive oil over medium-high heat. Stir in shrimp shells and sauté until pink. Add onion, celery, carrot, scallion, and garlic; stir. Add peppercorns, bay leaves, salt, and pepper; mix well. Add wine and bouquet garni.

2. Remove pot from heat. Add 4 cups water (or enough to fill the pot). Return to heat and bring to a boil. Stir and reduce heat to a simmer. Simmer for 20 minutes. Strain stock, discarding shrimp shells, seasonings, and vegetables.

G'S NOTES

Bouquet garni is a French term that refers to a bundle of herbs. A traditional bouquet garni includes parsley, thyme, and bay leaf and is most often tied in cheesecloth to make the herbs easier to retrieve and discard at the end of cooking.

meat lover's stew
makes/8 to 10 servings • see photo, page 108

¼ cup olive oil

8 ounces boneless, skinless
  chicken breast, chopped

3 tablespoons chopped garlic

2 tablespoons chopped shallot

1 teaspoon salt

1 teaspoon black pepper

8 ounces beef sirloin steak, cubed

8 ounces lamb, cubed

2 large potatoes, cubed

3 tablespoons curry powder

3 carrots, diced small

2 zucchini, sliced

1 yellow bell pepper, diced small

1 onion, diced small

8 ounces Italian sausage, sliced

5 cloves garlic

6 cups water

1 cup white wine

1 cup beef stock

1 cup halved grape tomatoes

8 ounces green peas
  (fresh or frozen)

1. In a large pot heat olive oil over medium heat. Add chicken, garlic, shallot, ½ teaspoon of the salt, and ½ teaspoon of the black pepper. Stir until chicken starts to brown.

2. Add steak, lamb, potato, and curry powder; mix well. Add carrot, zucchini, yellow pepper, and onion; stir. Stir in the sausage, garlic, the remaining ½ teaspoon salt, and ½ teaspoon black pepper. Pour in water, wine, and beef stock; stir.

3. Bring to a simmer. Add grape tomato halves and peas. Reduce heat. Cover and simmer for 20 to 30 minutes or until vegetables are tender. Stir and let sit for 5 minutes.

paella
makes/6 to 8 servings

¼ cup olive oil
2 tablespoons chopped garlic
2 tablespoons chopped shallot
¾ pound clams
¾ pound black mussels
3 medium lobster claws, raw
   and cracked
4 cups chicken stock
1 pound boneless, skinless
   chicken breast, diced small
1 teaspoon saffron
2 teaspoons turmeric powder
1 cup diced red bell pepper
2 stalks celery, diced small
2 carrots, diced small
½ cup diced white onion
8 ounces medium shrimp, peeled
   and deveined
8 ounces scallops
2 teaspoons salt
1 teaspoon black pepper
2 cups uncooked rice
1 cup water

1. In a paella pan or large skillet heat olive oil over medium heat. Add garlic and shallot; sauté for 1 minute or until slightly browned. Add clams, mussels, and lobster claws. Stir and let steam for 5 minutes.

2. Add chicken stock, chicken breast, saffron, and turmeric; mix well. Stir in bell pepper, celery, carrot, onion, shrimp, scallops, salt, and black pepper. Add rice and water; mix well. Bring to a boil; reduce heat. Cover and simmer about 25 minutes or until rice is tender.

chapter three

market
fresh

{ From garden salads to grilled salmon,
eating healthy can be so delicious. }

I have a question for you: Would you put sugar water in your gas tank, or would you run your favorite shoes through a car wash? So why would you put anything that is not of great quality into your body? Good food doesn't need to be an expensive chore, just one that takes a little more time when you are doing your shopping. When you take control of what you're buying, taking control of what you eat becomes so much easier. And remember the second rule of healthy living: Exercise your mind and muscles. Okay, don't be scared. Changing any bad habit—including the foods you choose—takes time, but you can do it. And always know that I got you back with deliciously healthy recipes and fresh cooking ideas.

spicy african salsa
makes/3 cups

1   pound okra
3   tablespoons olive oil
1   shallot, chopped
1   garlic clove, chopped
1   cup chicken stock
½   cup cooked black eyed peas
¼   cup diced tomato
¼   cup diced green bell pepper
¼   cup diced yellow bell pepper
¼   cup diced red bell pepper
1   Scotch bonnet pepper,
    seeded and diced
    (see tip, page 207)
½   teaspoon salt
½   teaspoon black pepper
2   tablespoons cider vinegar
1   tablespoon chopped
    fresh cilantro
1   teaspoon sugar

1. Wash okra and remove the tips and stems. Cut into 1-inch rounds; set aside.

2. In a sauté pan heat 1 tablespoon of the olive oil over medium heat. Stir in shallot and garlic. Add okra and sauté for 2 to 3 minutes or until tender. Add the chicken stock; simmer until all the liquid is absorbed. Remove from heat and set aside to cool.

3. In a bowl combine the black-eyed peas, tomato, and bell and Scotch bonnet peppers. Stir in okra mixture. Season with salt and black pepper.

4. In a separate bowl whisk together the remaining 2 tablespoons olive oil, the cider vinegar, cilantro, and sugar. Add to salsa; stir to combine.

mom's vegetable medley
makes/4 to 6 servings

1	tablespoon unsalted butter
4	cloves garlic, chopped
1	small onion, sliced
2	yellow squash, sliced
½	head broccoli, cut into florets
½	head cauliflower, cut into florets
½	pint mushrooms, sliced
3	plum tomatoes, diced
¼	cup water
1	cube chicken bouillon
	Salt
	Black pepper

1. In a large sauté pan melt butter over medium heat. Add garlic; sauté for 2 to 3 minutes or until garlic starts to turn brown. Add onion and cook for 3 minutes.

2. Add yellow squash, broccoli, cauliflower, mushrooms, and tomato. Cook and stir for 3 minutes more. Stir in water, bouillon, and salt and pepper to taste. Simmer until bouillon is dissolved.

yam, sweet potato, and apple **casserole**
makes/10 to 12 servings

3 **large yams**
3 **large sweet potatoes**
4 **Red Delicious apples**
  Margarine
½ **cup raisins**
¾ **cup honey**
¼ **cup orange juice**
2 **tablespoons ground cinnamon**
2 **tablespoons vanilla**
½ **cup powdered sugar**

1. Preheat oven to 350°F. Peel yams and potatoes. Place yams and potatoes in a large pot of water. Bring to a boil; reduce heat. Boil gently until yams and potatoes are tender. Remove yams and potatoes from water. When cool enough to handle, slice into rounds. Set aside. Peel, core, and slice apples.

2. Grease a 13×9×2 inch baking dish with margarine. Alternately arrange yam, sweet potato, and apple slices in a row on one side of the dish. Make two more rows. Top with raisins.

3. To make a glaze, in a small pan stir together honey, orange juice, cinnamon, and vanilla. Heat and stir over low heat until consistency is even. Pour glaze over yam, sweet potato, and apple slices.

4. Bake, uncovered, for 10 to 15 minutes or until browned. Remove from oven and sprinkle with powdered sugar. Serve immediately.

southern-style **string beans**

makes/4 servings

Salt
Black pepper
1 **pound French green beans**
1 **tablespoon unsalted butter**
1 **teaspoon chopped garlic**
1 **teaspoon chopped shallot**

1. Bring a small pot of water to a boil; season water with salt and pepper or your favorite seasoning.

2. Place green beans in water and cook for 12 to 15 minutes or until tender. Remove beans from pot and place in ice water. Drain and set aside.

3. In a sauté pan melt butter over medium heat. Add garlic and shallot; sauté lightly. Add string beans, turning to coat. Season with salt and pepper to taste. Serve string beans as a side dish.

G's NOTES
For the best results, make the water is boiling before you add the beans.

cherry tomato **salad**
makes/4 to 6 servings

1   bunch asparagus
2   tablespoons olive oil
1   cup red cherry tomatoes,
      cut in half
1   cup yellow pear tomatoes,
      cut in half
¼   cup finely sliced fresh basil
2   tablespoons chopped shallot
2   tablespoons chopped garlic
      Citrus Vinaigrette 1 (see recipe,
      below)
4   ounces goat cheese (chèvre)
      Balsamic vinegar
      French baguette slices,
      lightly toasted

1. Blanch the asparagus by placing spears in boiling water for approximately 45 seconds. Remove asparagus, then place in ice water. Drain well.

2. In a grill pan heat olive oil over high heat. Grill blanched asparagus about 2 minutes or until asparagus has grill marks. Place grilled asparagus on a cutting board and cut into bite-size pieces.

3. In a large bowl place asparagus, cherry tomato, yellow tomato, basil, shallot, and garlic; toss to combine. Add Citrus Vinaigrette 1 and toss to coat.

4. Place salad on serving plates. Crumble goat cheese over top. Drizzle salads with balsamic vinegar and top with toasted baguette slices.

 'S NOTES
When slicing tomatoes for salads and sandwiches, stand them with the stem pointing up and slice vertically. They will retain their juices better.

citrus vinaigrette 1
makes/about 1¼ cups • serve with cherry tomato salad

½   cup olive oil
½   cup orange juice
2   tablespoons lemon juice
1   teaspoon chopped garlic
1   teaspoon chopped shallot
1   teaspoon salt
1   teaspoon black pepper
1   tablespoon finely
      sliced fresh basil

1. In a bowl place olive oil, orange juice, lemon juice, garlic, shallot, salt, and pepper. Whisk until evenly mixed. Stir in basil.

tuna niçoise salad

makes/4 servings

2 3-ounce pieces tuna loin
2 teaspoons salt
2 teaspoons black pepper
9 tablespoons olive oil
2 tablespoons balsamic vinegar
1 teaspoon + 1 tablespoon
   chopped garlic
2 teaspoons chopped shallot
1 16-ounce package romaine,
   iceberg, and butter lettuce mix
1 6-ounce bunch string
   beans, blanched
¼ cup pitted kalamata olives
¼ cup sliced cooked potato
6 cornichon pickles, chopped
2 tablespoons capers
4 cherry tomatoes, halved
2 boiled eggs, halved

1. Season tuna with 1 teaspoon of the salt and 1 teaspoon of the pepper. In a grill pan heat 5 tablespoons of the olive oil over medium heat. Add tuna and sear until browned on both sides. Remove tuna from pan and set aside.

2. In a large glass bowl whisk together the remaining 4 tablespoons olive oil, balsamic vinegar, 1 teaspoon of the garlic, and 1 teaspoon of the shallot. Add lettuce mix and toss to coat. Place lettuce mix in center of a serving platter.

3. In another bowl place string beans, olives, potato, cornichon pickle, capers, the remaining 1 tablespoon garlic, and the remaining 1 teaspoon each of shallot, salt, and pepper; mix together. Spoon bean mixture onto plate with lettuce.

4. Slice tuna and place on top of lettuce. Top with tomato and egg halves. If desired, drizzle with additional balsamic vinegar.

seafood salad
makes/4 servings

5 tablespoons olive oil
3 Manila clams, scrubbed
6 black mussels, scrubbed
1 cup white wine
1 teaspoon chopped garlic
1 teaspoon chopped shallot
1 teaspoon salt
1 teaspoon black pepper
4 large shrimp, peeled
   and deveined
4 scallops
5 ounces calamari, cut into rings
1 cup canned sweet corn, drained
1 cup canned cannellini beans,
   rinsed and drained
½ cup sliced scallion
1 tablespoon chopped
   fresh parsley
½ avocado, peeled and sliced
3 teaspoons lemon juice

1. In a large sauté pan heat 1 tablespoon of the olive oil over medium heat. Add clams and mussels; sauté until shells open. Add wine, garlic, shallot, salt, and pepper; stir. Let simmer until wine is reduced by half.

2. Season shrimp, scallops, and calamari with additional salt and pepper. In a grill pan heat 1 tablespoon of the olive oil over medium-high heat. Place seafood mixture on grill pan. Flip from side to side until done. Set aside.

3. In pot place 1 tablespoon of the olive oil, the sweet corn, beans, scallion, and parsley. Sauté for 3 to 5 minutes, then place into large bowl. To the bowl add avocado slices, 1 tablespoon of the olive oil, and 1½ teaspoons of the lemon juice. Stir to coat.

4. Spoon corn mixture onto serving dishes. Top with clams, mussels, shrimp, scallops, and calamari.

5. For dressing, pour the pan sauce from the clam and mussel mixture into a bowl. Add the remaining 1 tablespoon olive oil, 1½ teaspoons lemon juice, and salt and pepper to taste. Mix together and pour over salad.

blackened chicken breast with papaya, peach, plum, and pineapple over mesclun greens

makes/4 servings • see photo, page 109

4	6-ounce boneless, skinless chicken breast halves
	Blackening Spice (see recipe, page 139)
2	tablespoons olive oil
1	peach, peeled, pitted, and diced
1	plum, peeled, pitted, and diced
1	papaya, peeled, pitted, and diced
½	pineapple, peeled, cored, and diced
1	teaspoon honey
1	teaspoon chopped fresh cilantro
1	teaspoon chopped fresh mint
12	ounces mesclun greens

1. Rinse chicken and pat dry. Season chicken with blackening spice.

2. In a sauté pan heat olive oil over medium heat. Add chicken and sauté for 3 to 4 minutes per side or until done. Remove from pan and set aside.

3. For salsa, in a medium bowl place all diced fruit, the honey, cilantro, and mint. Combine thoroughly. Place mesclun greens on serving plates. Top with chicken. Top chicken with fruit salsa.

G's NOTES
Peel and pit all fruit prior to assembling salsa.

whole wheat pasta with chicken and garden vegetables in a creamy wine and neufchâtel sauce

makes/4 to 6 servings

4 tablespoons olive oil
Salt
1 pound boneless, skinless
chicken breast
Black pepper
1 tablespoon chopped garlic
1 tablespoon chopped shallot
16 ounces whole wheat pasta
(desired shape)
1 small onion, diced
1 small green bell pepper, diced
1 yellow tomato, diced
1 red tomato, diced
2 ounces fresh baby spinach
½ cup chicken stock
½ cup Chardonnay wine
2 tablespoons low-fat cream
cheese (Neufchâtel)

1. Bring a pot of water to a boil. Add 3 tablespoons of the olive oil and a pinch of salt.

2. Meanwhile, slice chicken crosswise and season with salt and pepper to taste. In a large sauté pan heat the remaining 1 tablespoon oil over medium heat. Add garlic and shallot; sauté for 2 minutes. Add chicken and cook until three-quarters done.

3. Add pasta to boiling water and stir. Cook according to package directions until desired tenderness.

4. While pasta cooks, add onion and bell pepper to pan with chicken; sauté further. Add tomato and spinach to pan; stir well to combine. Add chicken stock and wine to pan; simmer for 2 minutes. Whisk in cream cheese until smooth.

5. Drain pasta and add to sauté pan. Toss to mix well.

chicken and broccoli with brown rice

makes/4 servings

8	tablespoons olive oil
2	tablespoons + 1 teaspoon chopped garlic
2	tablespoons + 1 teaspoon chopped shallot
1	cup uncooked brown rice
1	cup chicken stock
1	cup water
	Salt
	Black pepper
1	bunch broccoli
4	6-ounce boneless, skinless chicken breast halves
2	tablespoons unsalted butter

1. In a sauté pan heat 3 tablespoons of the olive oil over medium heat. Add 1 teaspoon each of the garlic and shallot; cook for 1 minute. Add rice; sauté for 2 minutes Stir in chicken stock, water, and a pinch each of the salt and pepper. Bring to a simmer; reduce heat. Cover and simmer for 25 minutes or until rice is tender. Set aside and keep warm.

2. Meanwhile, in a large pot bring 3 quarts of water to a boil. Add broccoli and boil for 5 to 7 minutes. Remove from pot and place in a bowl or sink of ice water. Drain well and cut into florets; set aside.

3. In a grill pan heat 3 tablespoons of the olive oil over medium heat. Season chicken with salt and pepper. Cook chicken in hot oil for 4 minutes per side or until golden brown. Set aside and keep warm.

4. In a frying pan heat the remaining 2 tablespoons oil and the butter over medium heat. Add the remaining 2 tablespoons garlic and 2 tablespoons shallot; mix well. Add broccoli florets; sauté for 2 minutes. Season with a pinch each of salt and pepper.

5. To serve, place chicken breasts on a serving platter. Add the broccoli and brown rice to platter.

stewed chicken with **basmati rice**

makes/4 servings

¼ cup + 1 tablespoon olive oil
1 whole chicken, cut into quarters
   Salt
   Black pepper
1 large onion, chopped
3 tablespoons chopped shallot
2 cups chicken stock
1 cup white wine
1 cup water
3 cups basmati rice
   Chopped fresh parsley

1. In a large stockpot heat ¼ cup of the olive oil over medium heat. Season chicken with salt and pepper. Brown chicken in hot oil until golden brown.

2. Add onion and shallot; cook for 3 to 5 minutes. Add chicken stock, white wine, and water. Let simmer for 15 to 20 minutes or until onion starts to break down.

3. Stir in rice. Cover pot and simmer for 15 minutes or until rice is tender, stirring every 5 minutes. Arrange chicken and rice on serving plate; garnish with parsley.

pan-seared turkey chops
makes/4 servings

2 tablespoons olive oil
8 3-ounce turkey chops,*
  ¼ inch thick
  Soul Food Seasoning (see recipe, below)
1 cup white wine
1 tablespoon unsalted butter

1. In a large sauté pan heat olive oil over medium heat. Rinse turkey chops. Season with Soul Food Seasoning, making sure to pat seasoning into meat to seal in flavor. Sear chops in hot pan for 9 to 12 minutes per side or until golden brown. (You may have to sear chops half at a time.) Remove chops from pan; lay on paper towels to soak up excess oil.

2. Add white wine to remaining juices in pan, stirring to loosen any browned bits from bottom of pan. Bring sauce to a slight simmer for 3 to 5 minutes; whisk in butter to finish.

3. To serve, place chops on a serving plate and drizzle sauce over chops.

* Turkey chops are also called turkey cutlets. They are ¼-inch-thick slices from the turkey breast. You can find them prepared in most supermarkets.

soul food seasoning
makes/about ⅔ cup

2 tablespoons red pepper flakes
2 tablespoons garlic powder
2 tablespoons onion powder
2 tablespoons dark chili powder
1 tablespoon paprika
1 tablespoon salt
1 teaspoon dried parsley
1 teaspoon ground thyme
1 teaspoon celery powder
1 pinch cayenne pepper

1. Pour all ingredients into a bowl. Mix together.

turkey **chili**
makes/6 to 8 servings

2 teaspoons olive oil
2 pounds lean ground turkey
1 cup chopped onion
2 cloves garlic, chopped
1 28-ounce can diced tomatoes
1 16-ounce can small red beans
½ cup diced red bell pepper
½ cup diced green bell pepper
1 tablespoon chopped
   jalapeño pepper
   (see tip, page 207)
2 teaspoons chili powder
½ teaspoon ground cumin
½ teaspoon salt
⅛ teaspoon black pepper
   Cooked rice (optional)
   Shredded cheddar cheese
   Sour cream
   Sliced scallion

1. In a Dutch oven or large roasting pan heat olive oil over medium heat. Add turkey, onion, and garlic. Cook until turkey is browned. Drain off fat.

2. Add undrained tomatoes, undrained red beans, bell pepper, jalapeno, chili powder, cumin, salt, and black pepper; stir to combine. Bring to a simmer; reduce heat. Cover and simmer for 25 to 30 minutes or until flavors are blended.

3. If desired, serve chili over rice. Top with cheddar cheese, sour cream, and scallion.

roasted lamb and arugula salad
with port wine reduction

makes/4 servings

2	8-ounce pieces lamb loin
5	tablespoons olive oil
1	teaspoon salt
½	teaspoon black pepper
1	cup red wine
½	cup port wine
¼	cup packed brown sugar
1	16-ounce bag baby arugula
¼	cup almonds, toasted
1	head Belgian endive
1	head radicchio
2	pears, cored and sliced*
⅓	cup crumbled feta cheese
2	teaspoons chopped shallot
2	teaspoons chopped garlic
	Pinch salt and black pepper

1. Preheat oven to 375°F. Coat lamb loin with 2 tablespoons of the oil. Season lamb on all sides with salt and pepper.

2. In a sauté pan heat 2 tablespoons of the olive oil over medium-high heat. Brown lamb on all sides in hot oil.

3. Place browned lamb in a roasting pan. Roast about 15 minutes or to desired doneness (145°F for medium rare). Remove lamb from oven and set aside.

4. In the same sauté pan add red wine, port wine, and brown sugar. Bring to a boil; reduce heat to very low. Simmer for 10 to 15 minutes or until liquid reduces and thickens. Remove reduction from heat and let cool. Drizzle some cooled reduction onto serving plates; set aside.

5. Place arugula in a large bowl. Add toasted almonds. Cut the bottoms off of the Belgian endive and radicchio; separate the leaves, then add to bowl. Add pear slices, feta, shallot, garlic, and a pinch each salt and pepper. Add the remaining 1 tablespoon olive oil. Toss salad so that it is mixed well.

6. Divide salad among serving plates. Drizzle additional wine reduction around outside of salad. Slice lamb loin diagonally into thin pieces; lay on top of salad. Drizzle remaining wine reduction over lamb and salad.

* Soak pear slices in a mixture of 1 cup water and 1 teaspoon lemon juice to prevent browning; drain.

grilled **atlantic salmon** with a vegetable medley
makes/4 servings

6   tablespoons olive oil
1   large eggplant, cubed
¼   cup ½ inch pieces red
      and orange bell pepper
¼   cup cubed green and yellow
      zucchini
¼   cup ½-inch pieces red onion
1   cup halved cherry tomatoes
1   16-ounce can plum
      tomatoes, drained
      Kosher salt
      Black pepper
2   tablespoons chopped garlic
2   tablespoons chopped shallot
3   tablespoons unsalted butter
2   tablespoons capers
2   tablespoons chopped
      fresh parsley
2   tablespoons lemon juice
2   8-ounce pieces salmon fillet
      (or four 4-ounce pieces)
4   ounces arugula

1. In a deep frying pan heat 2 tablespoons of the olive oil over medium heat. Add eggplant, bell pepper, zucchini, and onion; sauté until soft. Add cherry tomatoes and let cook for 1 minute. Add canned tomatoes and mix well. Add 2 tablespoons of the olive oil, a pinch of salt, and a pinch of black pepper.

2. Add the garlic and shallot; mix well and let simmer for 2 minutes. Stir in the butter, capers, parsley, and lemon juice; mix well and let cook until all vegetables are tender but not mushy.

3. In a grill pan heat the remaining 2 tablespoons olive oil over medium heat. Season the salmon with salt and black pepper. Grill salmon for 4 minutes per side or until firm but moist and fish starts to separate when you press down on it.

4. To serve, scoop vegetables onto a large serving plate and place salmon on top. Place arugula on top of salmon. Drizzle with additional olive oil and season to taste with salt and black pepper.

lobster, papaya, and mango
salad with citrus vinaigrette

makes/4 servings

2	**lobster tails, halved**
⅓	**cup + 4 tablespoons olive oil**
2	**teaspoons salt**
2	**teaspoons black pepper**
2	**large oranges**
¼	**cup orange juice**
2	**tablespoons rice wine vinegar**
2	**tablespoons lemon juice**
1	**teaspoon chopped garlic**
1	**teaspoon chopped shallot**
1	**papaya, peeled and sliced**
1	**mango, peeled and sliced**
4	**ounces mixed greens**

1. Coat lobster tails with 2 tablespoons of the olive oil. Season with 1 teaspoon each of the salt and pepper. In a grill pan heat 2 tablespoons of the olive oil over medium heat. Place lobster tails, flesh sides down, on the grill pan and cook for 2 to 6 minutes. Remove from pan and let cool.

2. Remove the peel from the oranges and cut out 12 segments; set aside. Into a medium bowl squeeze the juice from the remaining portions of the oranges. Add the ¼ cup orange juice, the rice wine vinegar, lemon juice, and the remaining ⅓ cup olive oil to bowl; whisk together. Whisk in garlic, shallot, and the remaining 1 teaspoon each salt and pepper. Set vinaigrette aside.

3. Remove shells from lobster tails. Place half a tail on each serving plate. Arrange orange segments, papaya, and mango next to lobster. Place mixed greens on top of the lobster, papaya, and mango. Drizzle vinaigrette over all. If desired, season with additional salt and pepper.

manila clams

makes/4 servings

¼ cup olive oil
2 pounds Manila clams*
2 cups halved cherry tomatoes
2 tablespoons chopped garlic
2 tablespoons chopped shallot
1½ teaspoons salt
1½ teaspoons black pepper
1 cup white wine
2 lemons, halved
8 pieces grilled asparagus
2 tablespoons chopped
    fresh parsley
2 tablespoons chopped
    fresh chives
2 tablespoons unsalted butter
  Toasted French baguette slices

1. In a large sauté pan heat olive oil over medium-high heat. Add clams (be careful of popping oil); move clams around in pan for about 1 minute.

2. Add tomatoes, garlic, shallot, salt, and pepper to pan. Stir to evenly cook tomatoes, garlic, and shallot. Pour in white wine and squeeze in juice from lemon halves. Let simmer for 3 to 5 minutes or until clams are open. Once clams have opened, add asparagus, parsley, and chives. Whisk in butter.

3. Remove clams and place on plates. Pour sauce over clams and top each serving with a toasted French baguette slice.

* Manila clams are smaller than the common littleneck clams.

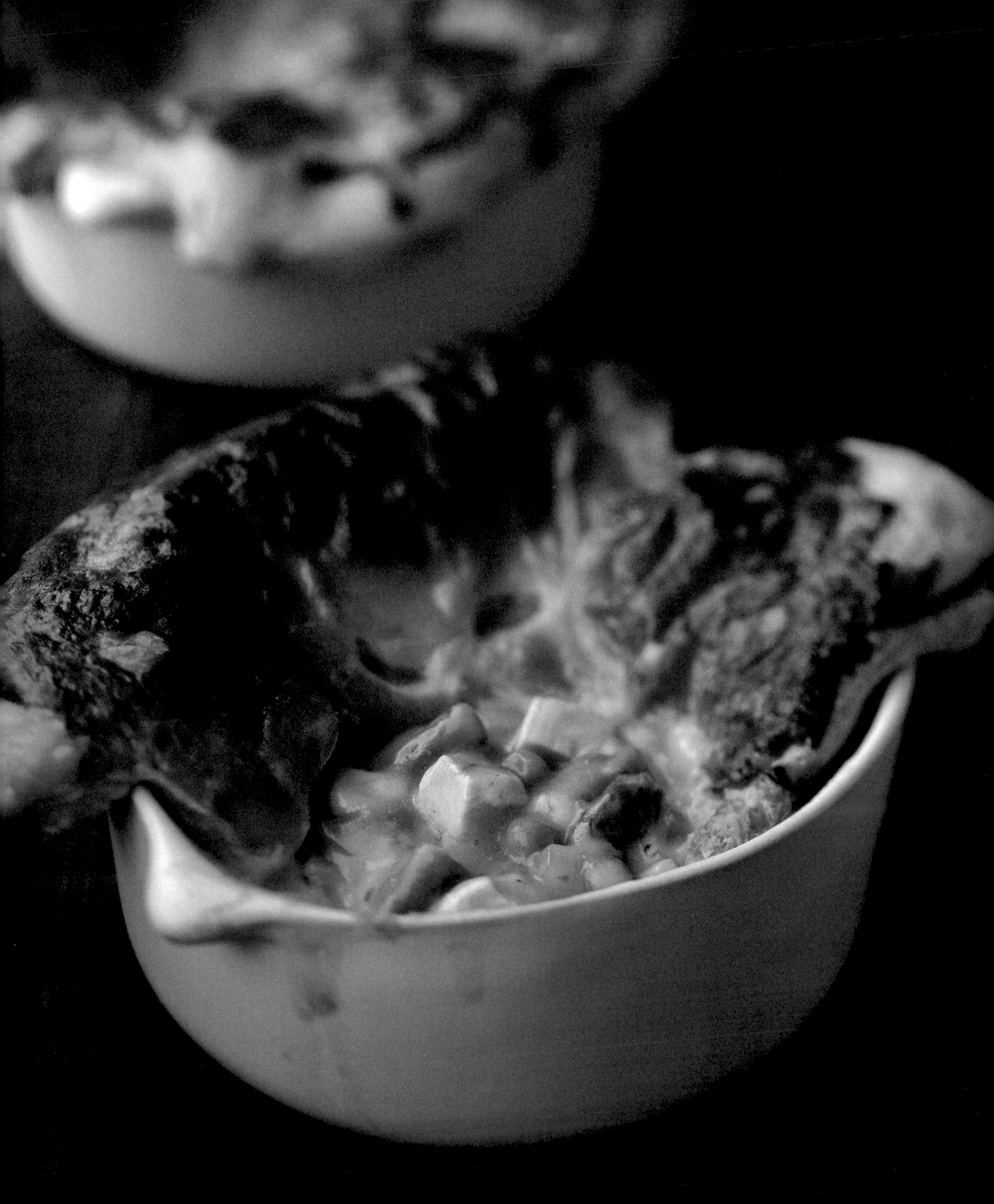

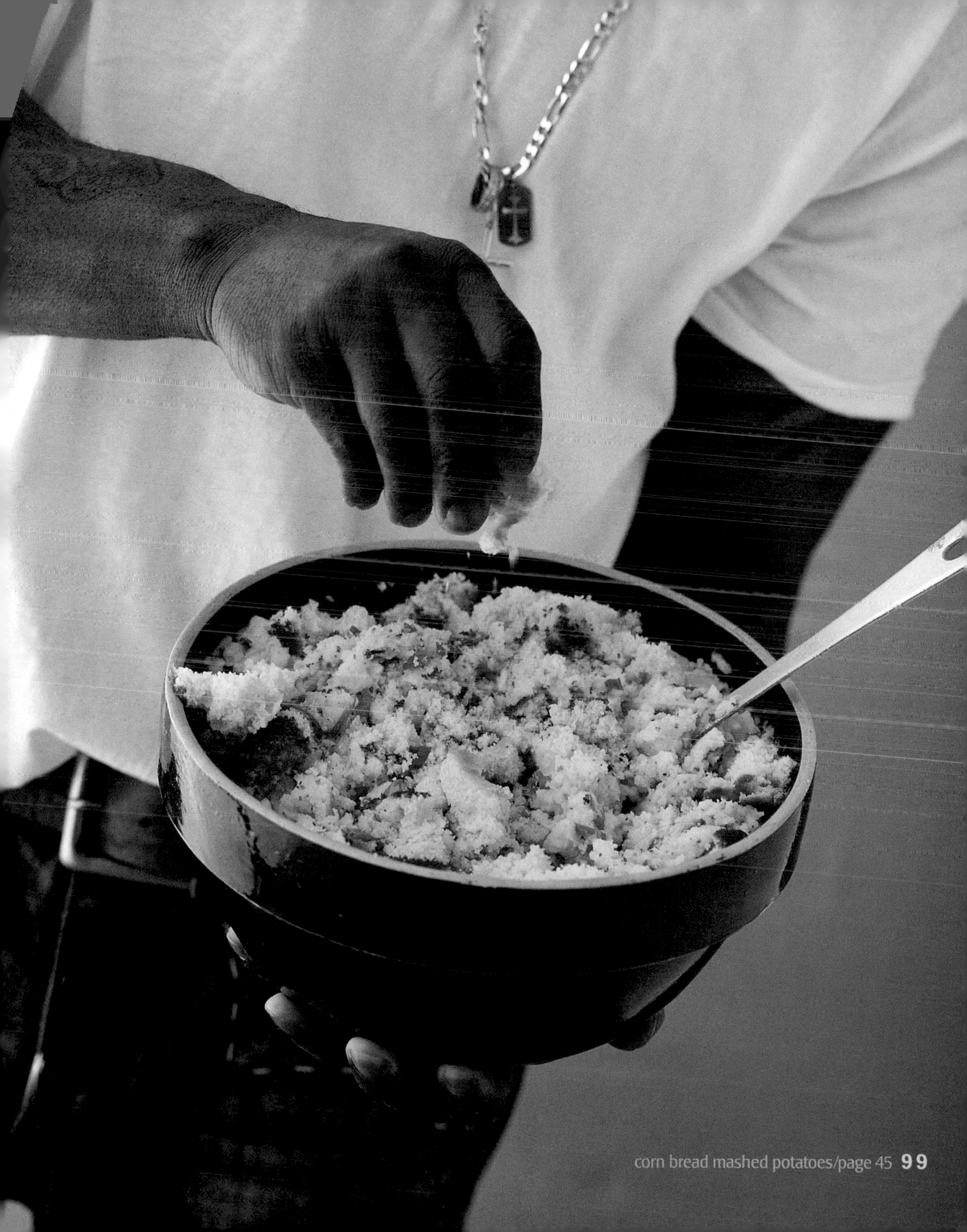

corn bread mashed potatoes/page 45

 chicken saté with spicy peanut sauce/page 13

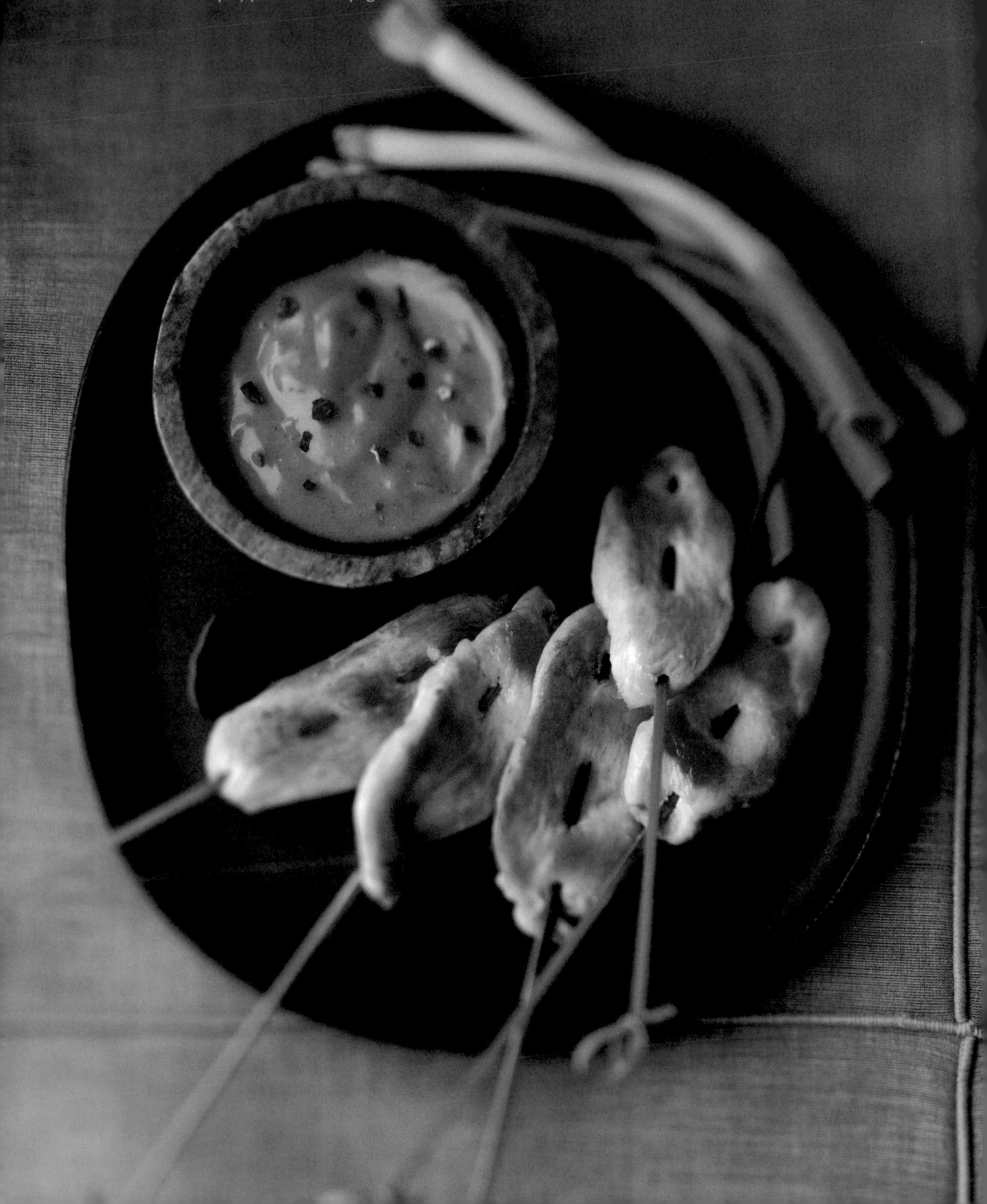

"My life has been a culinary journey and it's taught me so much about food and life. I now share with you the recipe of my life."

— Chef G. Garvin

 seafood bouillabaisse/page 71

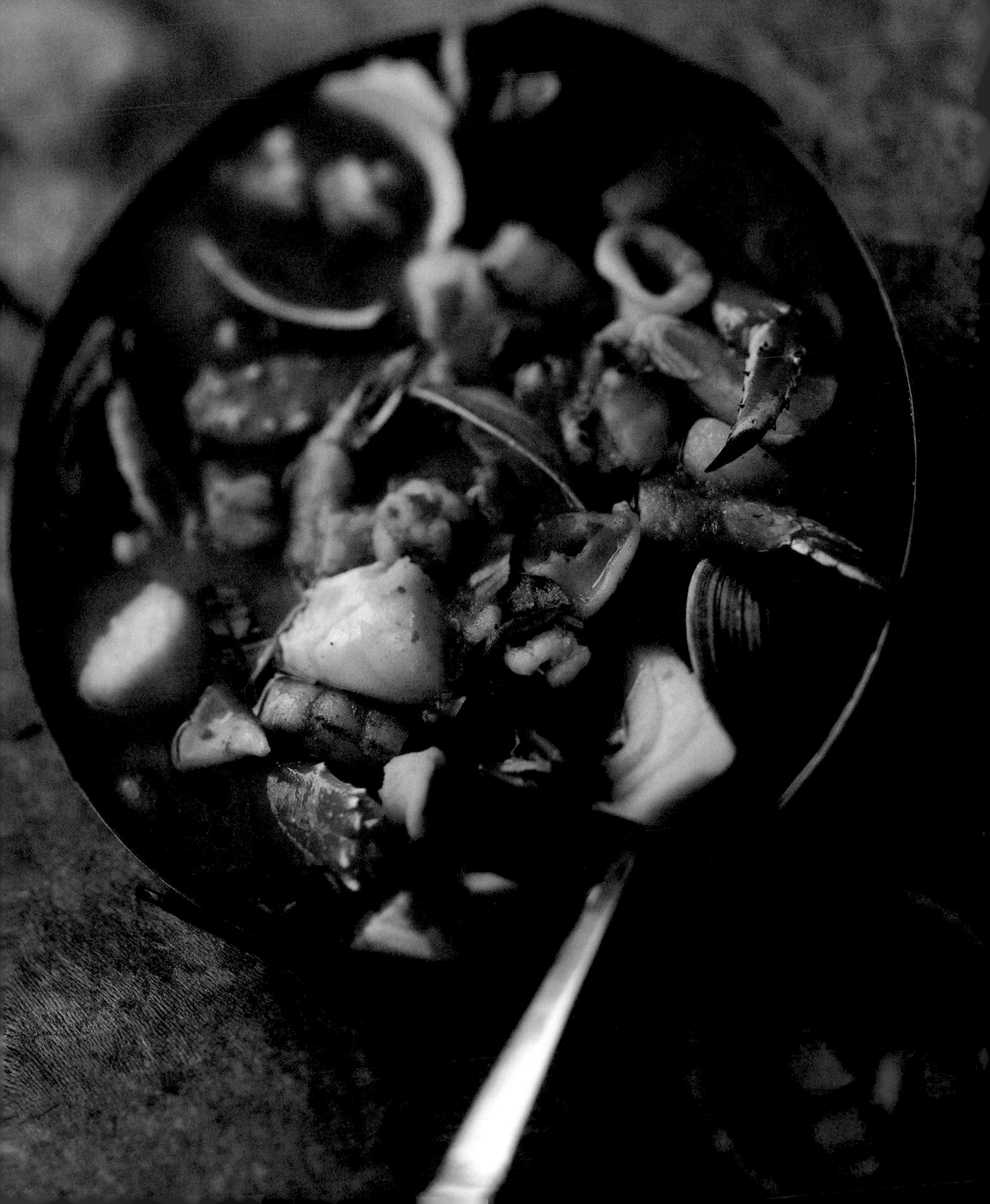

lobster, avocado, and brie omelet/page 117

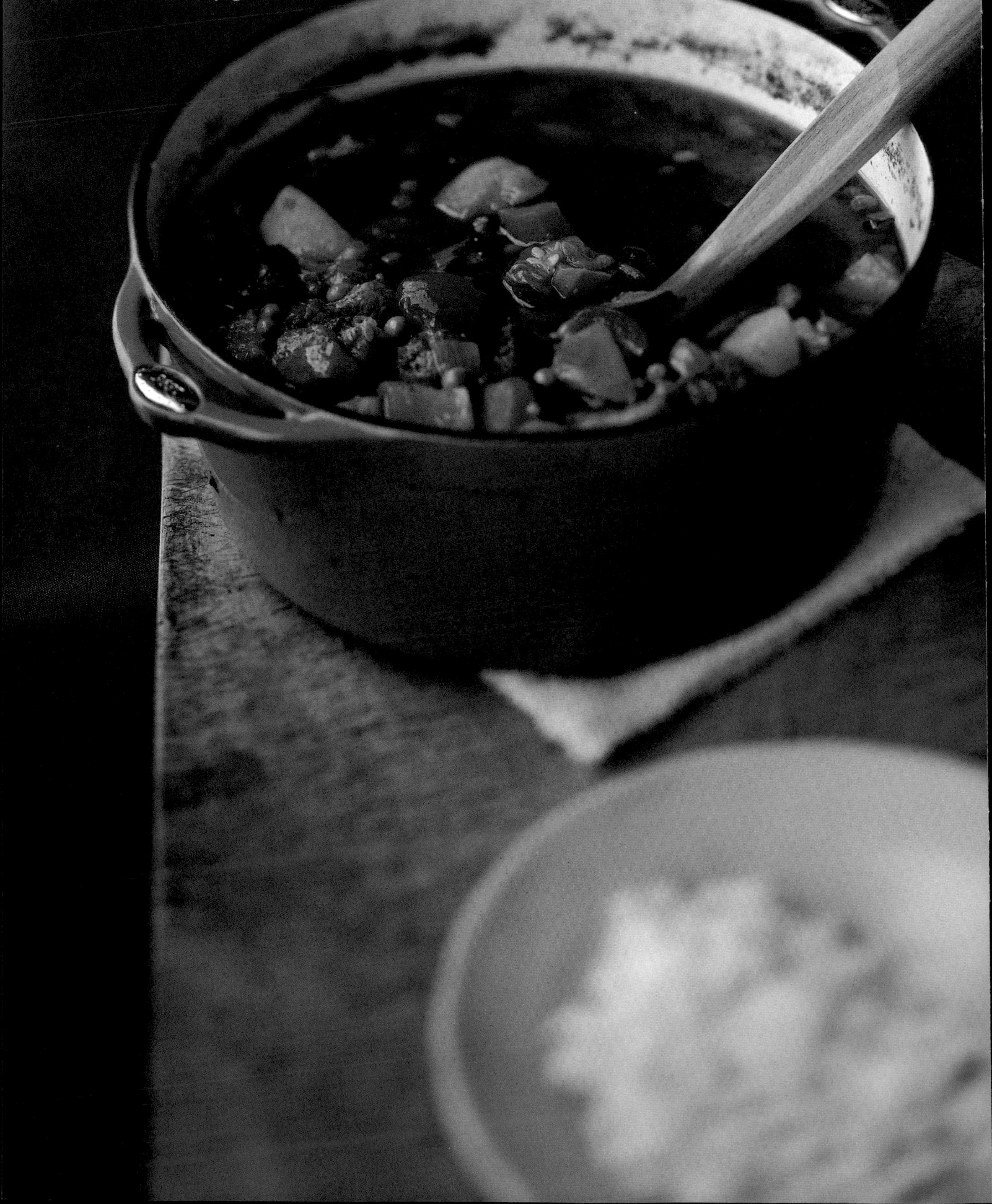

FRESH
HOT OR COLD
APPLE CIDER
$1.00 CUP

FUJI

Mutsu
(crispin)

yellow bell pepper purée soup and red bell pepper purée soup/pages 124–125 **111**

chapter four

good food
made
at home

{ Stay in tonight and whip up your own
gourmet dinner. No reservation needed. }

We all know how easy it is to go out to dinner because we all do it. There is nothing wrong with eating out, if that's your thing. Please believe me though, when you do decide to make home-cooked, when you make that run to the market, pick up some fresh produce, some superfresh seafood, or a couple of good steaks, the experience becomes more than just dinner out at some restaurant. Everyone can take part in the preparation. While cooking, open a bottle of wine. Play some tunes, you know, maybe some Musiq Soul Child, Anthony Hamilton, or Mariah Carey. Whatever you enjoy. But remember, this is what it is all about: Good times and good food, keeping it real and keeping it smooth—all at the house.

eggs benedict with crab and spicy creole mustard
makes/4 servings

3 tablespoons olive oil
½ cup crabmeat
1 tablespoon chopped garlic
1 tablespoon chopped shallot
1 teaspoon butter
2 whole egg buns or English
   muffins, split in half
4 large eggs
   Spicy Creole Mustard
     (see recipe, below)

1. In a frying pan heat 1 tablespoon of the olive oil over medium heat. Add crabmeat, garlic, and shallot; mix well. Set aside.

2. In another frying pan heat 1 tablespoon of the olive oil and the butter over medium heat. Place egg buns, cut sides down, in pan. Cook for 2 to 3 minutes or until golden brown and buns are warmed through. Place toasted buns on plates and set aside.

3. Heat the remaining 1 tablespoon olive oil in the same pan over medium heat. Crack eggs directly into the pan and let cook for approximately 2 minutes. Turn eggs over and continue to cook for 2 minutes more or until eggs are cooked to your liking.

4. To serve, place crab mixture on top of toasted egg buns. Top the crab mixture with the eggs. Drizzle Spicy Creole Mustard on top.

spicy creole mustard: Place 2 egg yolks, 1 tablespoon lemon juice, 2 tablespoons Dijon mustard, and 2 tablespoons hot sauce in a mixing bowl; whisk briskly. Add a pinch each of Old Bay® seasoning and black pepper; mix well. Slowly add ½ cup olive oil while rapidly whisking. Add a pinch each of salt and chopped fresh parsley; mix well.

french toast with warm maple syrup and fresh berries

makes/4 servings

2 eggs
¼ cup heavy cream
1 tablespoon vanilla extract
1 teaspoon cinnamon
1 tablespoon powdered sugar
¼ cup olive oil
1 cup maple syrup
4 slices potato bread (double-thick slices may also be used)
8 ounce fresh mixed berries (strawberries, blueberries, any of your favorites)
Powdered sugar

1. In a medium bowl whisk together eggs and cream. Add vanilla and cinnamon; mix well. Add 1 tablespoon powdered sugar and whisk until dissolved.

2. In a skillet heat olive oil over medium heat. In a saucepan heat maple syrup over low heat.

3. Dip bread in the egg batter, making sure both sides are coated. Place bread in hot skillet. Cook for 3 minutes per side or until golden brown.

4. To serve, place French toast on a plate; cut in half and drizzle with warm syrup. Garnish plate with fresh berries. Sprinkle entire dish with additional powdered sugar.

lobster, avocado, and **brie omelet**

makes/1 large or 2 small servings* • see photo, page 107

1	**tablespoon olive oil**
6	**ounces cooked lobster, diced**
1	**tablespoon chopped garlic**
1	**tablespoon chopped shallot**
3	**large eggs**
¼	**cup milk**
1	**teaspoon salt**
1	**teaspoon black pepper**
¼	**cup sliced Brie cheese**
¼	**avocado, sliced**
1	**teaspoon chopped fresh parsley (optional)**

1. In a nonstick frying pan heat olive oil over medium heat. Add lobster, garlic, and shallot to pan. Let cook for 2 to 3 minutes so lobster can absorb the garlic and shallot flavors.

2. In a large bowl combine eggs, milk, salt, and pepper; beat vigorously. Pour egg mixture into pan. Let cook for 3 to 5 minutes, tilting pan and lifting eggs to let uncooked portion flow underneath.

3. Top eggs with Brie and avocado. Fold omelet in half. Gently slide omelet onto a plate. If desired, garnish with parsley.

G's NOTES

For cooking omelets, invest in a high-temperature rubber spatula. This spatula will resist melting at high heat. Look for them at your local restaurant supply store, housewares store, or grocery store.

blackened **snapper**
makes/4 servings

½ cup olive oil
4 8-ounce red snapper fillets,
     skin removed
2 tablespoons Blackening Spice
     (see recipe, page 139)

1. In a frying pan heat olive oil over medium heat. Season snapper fillets with blackening spice, patting spice into fish. Cook fillets in hot oil for 3 to 4 minutes per side or until golden. Place fillets on paper towels to absorb excess oil.

three-cheese scrambled eggs
makes/4 servings • serve with blackened snapper

4 eggs
½ cup heavy cream
     Salt
     Black pepper
2 teaspoons + 1 teaspoon
     unsalted butter
¼ cup shredded provolone cheese
¼ cup shredded Monterey
     Jack cheese
¼ cup shredded mozzarella cheese
6 to 8 scallions, chopped

1. Crack eggs into a medium bowl; whisk until smooth. Whisk in cream and season with salt and pepper. In a nonstick frying pan melt 2 teaspoons butter over medium heat. Pour egg mixture into pan. Cook, stirring constantly, until eggs are bright yellow and fluffy. Stir in 1 teaspoon butter,. Add cheeses and scallion; mix well.

home **fries**

makes/4 servings • serve with blackened snapper

2 large russet potatoes,
   peeled and cubed
¼ cup olive oil
1 tablespoon unsalted butter
2 tablespoons chopped garlic
2 tablespoons chopped shallot
1 bunch scallions, sliced
1½ teaspoons chopped fresh
   rosemary
1 teaspoons chopped
   fresh thyme
½ teaspoon salt
½ teaspoon black pepper

1. In a large pot bring 3 quarts of water to a boil. Add potato and boil for 6 to 8 minutes. (Potato cubes should not be completely done.) Drain and rinse potato cubes under cold water. Drain well.

2. In a large frying pan heat olive oil and butter over medium heat. Add garlic and shallot; sauté for 30 seconds. Add potato and mix well. Add scallion, rosemary, thyme, salt, and pepper. Cook until potato is tender, stirring occasionally.

G's NOTES

If you'd like, add chopped red or yellow bell pepper to the frying pan with the potato.

crab-stuffed baby portobello mushrooms

makes/10 appetizers

¼   cup + 1 tablespoon olive oil
1   tablespoon unsalted butter
1   tablespoon chopped garlic
1   tablespoon chopped shallot
10   baby portobello mushrooms,
      washed and stemmed
      Salt
      Black pepper
1   tablespoon chopped red
      bell pepper
1   tablespoon chopped orange
      bell pepper
1   tablespoon chopped green
      bell pepper
8   ounces lump crabmeat
1½   teaspoons hot sauce
1½   teaspoons Worcestershire
      sauce
2   tablespoons mayonnaise
2   tablespoons Dijon mustard
2   teaspoons Old Bay® seasoning
½   cup bread crumbs

1. Preheat oven at 350°F. In a large sauté pan heat ¼ cup olive oil and the butter over medium heat. Add garlic and shallot; sauté for 2 minutes. Add mushrooms and season to taste with salt and black pepper; sauté for 2 minutes more. Remove from heat. Place mushrooms, stem sides down, on a sheet pan lined with parchment paper; set aside.

2. In the same pan heat the remaining 1 tablespoon olive oil over medium heat. Add the bell pepper. Sauté for 1 minute; set aside to cool.

3. In a medium bowl combine crabmeat, hot sauce, Worcestershire sauce, mayonnaise, mustard, Old Bay seasoning, and a pinch each of salt and black pepper; mix well. Stir in sautéed bell pepper. Spoon crab mixture into mushrooms. Sprinkle tops with bread crumbs. Bake for 10 minutes or until bread crumbs are golden brown.

jalapeño **seafood dip**
makes/8 to 10 appetizer servings

1 pound cooked crabmeat
8 ounces cooked lobster
8 ounces cooked shrimp
1 cup shredded Monterey
    Jack cheese
6 tablespoons mayonnaise
¼ cup shredded cheddar cheese
¼ cup grated Parmesan cheese
2 tablespoons chopped garlic
2 teaspoons hot sauce
2 teaspoons Worcestershire sauce
1 teaspoon chopped jalapeño
    pepper (see tip, page 207)
1 teaspoon salt
1 teaspoon black pepper
    Assorted chips or crackers

1. Preheat oven to 350°F. Place all ingredients, except chips, in a bowl; mix well. Place seafood mixture in a medium baking dish. Bake, uncovered, about 15 minutes or until browned. Serve with chips.

bartlett pear salad with mixed greens

makes/4 servings

- 5 tablespoons unsalted butter
- 7 tablespoons packed brown sugar
- 4 tablespoons honey
- 1 cup chopped walnuts
- 2 large Bartlett pears
- 1 cup water
  Pinch ground cinnamon
  Pinch ground nutmeg
- 8 endive leaves
- 8 ounces mixed baby greens
- ¼ cup crumbled blue cheese
- 2 tablespoons Dijon mustard
- 2 tablespoons balsamic vinegar
- ½ cup olive oil
- 1 tablespoon chopped garlic
- 1 teaspoon chopped shallot
  Salt
  Black pepper

1. In a saucepan melt butter over low heat. Add 4 tablespoons of the brown sugar and 2 tablespoons of the honey; stir until sugar melts. Stir in walnuts until coated with brown sugar mixture. Spread coated walnuts on a baking sheet lined with parchment paper. Set aside to let walnuts cool and harden.

2. Preheat oven to 325°F. Peel pears, cut each in half, and remove cores. Place pear halves, cut sides down, in a baking dish. Add water, cinnamon, nutmeg, 1 tablespoon of the brown sugar, and the remaining 2 tablespoons honey to pears. Cover dish with foil. Bake for 30 to 35 minutes or until pears are tender but still firm.

3. Let baked pears cool. Place in a circle on a serving plate. Place endive leaves between pear halves. (Alternate pear half, endive leaf, pear half, etc.) Arrange mixed greens in center of plate. Top with blue cheese and sugared walnuts.

4. For vinaigrette, in a small bowl combine Dijon mustard, balsamic vinegar, and the remaining 2 tablespoons brown sugar; mix well. Add olive oil; mix well. Stir in garlic and shallot.

5. Drizzle vinaigrette over the entire salad. Season to taste with salt and pepper.

G's NOTES

Instead of using the balsamic vinaigrette recipe here, Citrus Vinaigrette 1 (see recipe, page 83) can be used.

rustic **roast potatoes**
makes/6 to 8 servings

1   **tablespoon salt**
4   **large Yukon gold potatoes**
     or your favorite variety
8   **ounces bacon**
4   **cups canola oil**
2   **cups shredded cheddar cheese**
     Salt
     Black pepper
1   **bunch scallions, sliced**

1. Preheat oven to 375°F. In a large pot combine 2 quarts water and 1 tablespoon salt; bring to a boil. Peel and roughly chop the potato. Add potato to boiling water and boil for 10 to 12 minutes or until three-quarters of the way done. Drain and let potato cool.

2. Chop the bacon and place in a medium sauté pan. Cook over medium heat until crispy. Drain off fat. Set aside.

3. In a large pot or deep fryer heat oil to 350°F. Add drained potato and fry until golden brown. Remove potato from oil and drain on paper towels to remove excess oil.

4. Transfer potato to an oven-safe serving platter. Sprinkle with cheese, bacon, and salt and pepper to taste. Place in the hot oven until cheese melts and is bubbly. Sprinkle with scallion.

yellow bell pepper purée soup
makes/6 to 8 servings • see photo, page 111

5 large yellow bell peppers
1 large white onion
2 stalks celery
2 tablespoons olive oil
2 to 3 cloves garlic, crushed
½ cup chopped shallot
2 teaspoons salt
1 teaspoon black pepper
8 cups chicken stock
¾ teaspoon saffron
1 cup heavy cream
   Toasted bread
     or dinner rolls

1. Cut bell peppers in half and remove seeds and ribs. Cut pepper, onion, and celery into ½-inch pieces. Set aside.

2. In a stockpot heat olive oil over medium-high heat. Add onion, celery, and garlic to pot; sauté for 2 to 3 minutes. Add bell pepper, shallot, salt, and black pepper to pot; sauté for 2 minutes. Add chicken stock and saffron to pot. Bring to a boil. Slowly add cream to pot; mix well. Remove from heat and cool slightly.

3. Pour lukewarm soup into a blender and purée until mixture is smooth. Strain soup through a medium-size strainer into a second pot. Warm soup over very low heat. Ladle soup into bowls and garnish with toast or rolls.

G's NOTES

The red and yellow pepper purée soups can be made in the same meal. Depending on which soup you want to be the base color, use the other soup to garnish. Place a spoonful of the garnish soup into the center of the base soup and use a toothpick to pull wisps of the garnish soup into the base soup. Thickened cream may be used to garnish the same way.

red bell pepper purée soup

makes/6 to 8 servings • see photo, page 111

5 large red bell peppers
1 large white onion
2 stalks celery
2 tablespoons olive oil
2 to 3 cloves garlic, crushed
½ cup chopped shallot
2 teaspoons salt
1 teaspoon black pepper
3 cups chicken stock
3 cups water
2 cups heavy cream
2 tablespoons tomato paste

1. Cut bell peppers in half and remove seeds and ribs. Cut pepper, onion, and celery into ½-inch pieces. Set aside.

2. In a stockpot heat olive oil over medium-high heat. Add onion, celery, and garlic to pot; sauté for 2 to 3 minutes. Add bell pepper, shallot, salt, and black pepper to the pot; sauté for 2 minutes. Add chicken stock and water to pot. Bring to a boil. Slowly add cream to pot. Stir in tomato paste; mix well. Remove from heat and cool slightly.

3. Pour lukewarm soup into a blender and purée until mixture is smooth. Strain soup through a medium-size strainer into a second pot. Warm soup over very low heat. Ladle soup into bowls.

curried coconut soup
makes/6 servings

2 tablespoons olive oil
1 large onion, diced small
1 tablespoon chopped garlic
1 tablespoon chopped shallot
½ Scotch bonnet pepper, seeded
   (see tip, page 207)
2 teaspoons curry powder
3½ cups coconut milk
   Salt
   White pepper
1½ cups chicken stock
2 teaspoons cornstarch
2 teaspoons water
½ cup plain yogurt
¼ cup unsweetened
   coconut, toasted
1 sprig fresh mint
1 tablespoon chopped
   fresh parsley

1. In a large pot heat olive oil over medium heat. Add onion, garlic, shallot, and Scotch bonnet; sauté until tender. Stir in curry powder. Next add coconut milk. Let simmer for 5 to 7 minutes. Season to taste with salt and white pepper.

2. Add chicken stock and bring to a simmer. Simmer for 5 minutes more. In a small bowl combine cornstarch and water to create a thickening agent. To finish soup, slowly add cornstarch mixture, whisking it in until smooth. Continue to simmer and slightly bubble for a minute or 2 more.

3. To serve, place a small spoonful each of yogurt, toasted coconut, mint, and parsley into bowls and ladle soup around, filling the bowls.

chicken marsala with angel
hair pasta and button mushrooms

makes/4 servings

6   tablespoons olive oil
2   teaspoons salt
4   boneless, skinless chicken
       breast halves
1   teaspoon black pepper
1   cup all-purpose flour
2   cups sliced button mushrooms
2   tablespoons chopped garlic
2   tablespoons chopped shallot
4   tablespoons unsalted butter
1   cup Marsala wine
1   cup heavy cream
12   ounces angel hair pasta

1. Fill a 6-quart stockpot with water; add 2 tablespoons of the olive oil and the salt. Bring to a boil.

2. Place chicken between two sheets of plastic wrap. Pound chicken with a mallet until it is almost flat. Discard plastic wrap. Season chicken with additional salt and the pepper.

3. In a sauté pan heat the remaining 4 tablespoons olive oil over medium-high heat. Place flour in a shallow dish; dredge chicken in flour. Sauté chicken in hot oil for 2 minutes per side. Add mushrooms, garlic, shallot, and 3 tablespoons of the butter; cook for 7 to 8 minutes or until chicken is firm and cooked through. Remove chicken from pan and set aside.

4. Add Marsala to the pan and let simmer. Next add cream and stir rapidly. Add salt and pepper to taste. Finish sauce by stirring in the remaining 1 tablespoon butter until melted. Return chicken to pan; let simmer for 2 minutes.

5. Place angel hair pasta in the pot of boiling water; cook for 3 to 4 minutes or to desired tenderness. Drain pasta and place on plates. Place chicken on pasta and top with Marsala sauce.

chicken parmesan
makes/4 servings

4 8-ounce boneless, skinless
  chicken breast halves
2 tablespoons garlic powder
2 tablespoons onion powder
2 tablespoons dried
  Italian seasoning
1 teaspoon salt
1 teaspoon black pepper
1 egg
½ cup heavy cream
2 cups dry bread crumbs*
¼ cup olive oil
8 ounces grated Parmesan cheese
8 ounces grated fresh
  mozzarella cheese
  Tomato Sauce (see recipe,
  opposite)
  Tri-Color Pasta (see recipe,
  opposite)

1. Preheat oven to 375°F. Season chicken with garlic powder, onion powder, Italian seasoning, salt, and pepper. In a shallow dish whisk together egg and cream. Place bread crumbs on a plate.

2. In a large skillet heat olive oil over medium heat. Dip chicken in egg mixture, then dredge in bread crumbs to coat. Brown chicken on both sides in hot skillet. Place browned chicken in a baking dish. Bake, uncovered, for 10 minutes.

3. Sprinkle cheeses over chicken and cover with Tomato Sauce. Bake for 5 minutes more or until cheese melts. Serve with Tri-Color Pasta.

* The bread crumbs can be seasoned with grated Parmesan cheese, if desired.

tomato sauce

makes/about 5 cups

¼ cup olive oil
2 teaspoons chopped garlic
  Pinch chopped shallot
1 teaspoon salt
½ teaspoon black pepper
1 16-ounce can peeled whole
    plum tomatoes
1 cup diced plum tomato
½ cup diced green bell pepper
½ cup diced red bell pepper
2 tablespoons tomato paste
2 whole cloves garlic
2 cups vegetable stock
2 tablespoons unsalted butter
2 teaspoons chopped fresh basil
1 cup white wine
2 tablespoons grated
    Parmesan cheese
2 teaspoons chopped
    fresh oregano
1 teaspoon chopped fresh thyme

1. In a large pot heat olive oil over medium-high heat. Add chopped garlic and shallot; sauté until soft. Stir in ½ teaspoon of the salt and the black pepper. Add all tomatoes and bell pepper; mix well. Add tomato paste and whole garlic; stir.

2. Use a handheld blender to chop whole tomatoes in pot; remove blender and stir. Add vegetable stock, butter, basil, and the remaining ½ teaspoon salt; stir. Stir in white wine. Cook for 5 minutes or until sauce comes to a boil. Stir in Parmesan cheese, oregano, and thyme.

tri-color pasta

makes/4 to 6 servings

3 tablespoons olive oil
1 teaspoon salt
1 teaspoon black pepper
1 16-ounce box tri-color pasta
3 tablespoons chopped garlic
3 tablespoons chopped shallot
1 tablespoon chopped fresh basil
1 tablespoon chopped
    fresh oregano
½ cup white wine
¼ cup chicken stock
1 cup chopped plum tomato
2 tablespoons capers

1. Bring a large pot of water to a boil. Add 1 tablespoon of the olive oil, the salt, and pepper. Add pasta and cook until tender but still firm (al dente). Drain; set aside.

2. In a large skillet heat the remaining 2 tablespoons olive oil over medium-high heat. Add garlic, shallot, basil, and oregano; mix well. Add the white wine and chicken stock. Bring to a boil. Stir in tomato and capers. Add cooked pasta to skillet and mix until all the pasta is coated.

shiitake mushroom **chicken ravioli**
makes/12 ravioli

3 tablespoons + 1 teaspoon
    olive oil
8 ounces boneless, skinless
    chicken breast, diced
    Salt
    Black pepper
½ cup sliced shiitake mushrooms
3 tablespoons goat
    cheese (chèvre)
1 tablespoon chopped garlic
1 tablespoon chopped shallot
1 large egg
¼ cup heavy cream
12 wonton wrappers
1 cup cornstarch
2 teaspoons unsalted butter
    Plum Tomato-White Wine Sauce
    (see recipe, opposite)
    Goat cheese and basil
    for garnish

1. Coat two skillets with 1 tablespoon each of the olive oil; heat over medium heat. Season chicken with a pinch each salt and pepper; add chicken to one skillet. Sauté chicken until cooked through. Place cooked chicken in a food processor and pulse until finely chopped but not pasty. Place in a medium bowl and set aside.

2. Meanwhile, add mushrooms to the second skillet and season lightly with salt and pepper. Sauté for 3 to 4 minutes or until tender. Place cooked mushrooms in food processor and pulse until finely chopped. Place in bowl with chicken.

3. In another bowl combine 3 tablespoons of the goat cheese, 1 teaspoon of the olive oil (to loosen cheese), the garlic, and shallot; set aside. In a small bowl beat egg and cream together until smooth; set aside.

4. In a large pot combine 2 quarts water, the remaining 1 tablespoon olive oil, and 1 tablespoon salt; bring to a boil over medium-high heat. Using a pastry brush, brush egg mixture onto a wonton wrapper. (Note: Place unused wonton wrappers between damp paper towels to keep them from drying out.)

5. Place some chicken mixture and cheese mixture from each bowl in the center wonton wrapper; be careful not to overload. Fold wonton into desired shape (triangle or rectangle), pressing edges with fingertips to seal. Once sealed, lightly dust ravioli with cornstarch so they do not stick when they are boiled. Repeat with remaining wrappers and fillings.

6. Add ravioli to the boiling water. Cook for 3 minutes or until they float and are tender but not mushy. With a slotted spoon, gently remove ravioli and place in a sauté pan over medium heat. Add butter to pan and stir. When butter is melted, remove ravioli and place on plate.

7. Serve Plum Tomato-White Wine Sauce over ravioli. You may garnish with additional goat cheese, basil, and freshly ground black pepper.

 G's NOTES

Be sure to make all of your ravioli at one time and place them on the side. If the water is boiling too rapidly, turn it down slightly. You don't want a hard boil or it will break your ravioli.

plum tomato-white wine sauce

makes/about 2 cups

¼ cup olive oil
1 tablespoon chopped garlic
1 tablespoon chopped shallot
1½ cups diced plum tomato
2 canned plum tomatoes, crushed
1 fresh basil leaf
¼ cup white wine
1 teaspoon salt
1 teaspoon black pepper
1 teaspoon chopped fresh
 Italian parsley
1 teaspoon unsalted butter

1. In a sauté pan heat the olive oil over medium heat. Add the garlic and shallot; sauté for 2 minutes. Stir in all the tomatoes. Add the basil leaf followed by the white wine and stir. Season sauce with salt, pepper, and parsley. Finish sauce by stirring in butter until melted. Serve over pasta.

chinese **chicken salad**
makes/4 servings

- 4 boneless, skinless chicken breast halves
- 2 tablespoons olive oil
- 1 teaspoon seasoned salt
- ½ teaspoon salt
- ½ teaspoon black pepper
- 1 head romaine lettuce
- 1 head butter lettuce
- ½ red bell pepper, thinly sliced
- ½ yellow bell pepper, thinly sliced
- 1 cup mandarin oranges
- ¼ cup almonds, toasted
- 6 wonton wrappers
- 1 cup canola oil
  Dijon Mustard and Miso Dressing (see recipe, below)
- 2 tablespoons pine nuts, toasted

1. Coat chicken breasts with the olive oil. Season chicken on both sides with seasoned salt, salt, and black pepper.

2. Heat a grill pan over medium-high heat. Grill chicken on both sides in hot pan until browned; remove from pan. Place chicken on paper towels to absorb excess oil. Slice chicken into small pieces; set aside.

3. Chop romaine and butter lettuce. Place chopped lettuce in a bowl with sliced chicken, bell pepper, mandarin oranges, and almonds.

4. Cut wonton wrappers into thin strips. In a sauté pan heat canola oil over medium-high heat. Place wonton strips in pan; fry until golden. Using a slotted spoon, remove strips from pan and place on paper towels to absorb excess oil.

5. Pour Dijon Mustard and Miso Dressing over salad and toss. Garnish salad with toasted pine nuts and fried wonton strips.

dijon mustard and **miso dressing**
makes/1¼ cups • serve with chinese chicken salad

- 2 tablespoons Dijon mustard
- 2 teaspoons miso
- ¼ cup soy sauce
- 2 tablespoons sesame oil
- 2 tablespoons packed brown sugar
- 2 tablespoons honey
- ½ cup olive oil
- 1 teaspoon sesame seeds
  Pinch chopped fresh parsley

1. In a medium bowl stir together Dijon mustard and miso. Stir in soy sauce, sesame oil, brown sugar, and honey. Whisk in olive oil, sesame seeds, and parsley.

stuffed pork chops with ricotta and spinach
makes/4 servings • see photo, page 177

2	tablespoons unsalted butter
¼	cup + 3 tablespoons olive oil
4	teaspoons chopped garlic
4	teaspoons chopped shallot
16	ounces spinach
2	teaspoons salt
2	teaspoons black pepper
⅓	cup grated Parmesan cheese
¼	cup ricotta cheese
4	bone-in pork chops (at least 1½ inches thick)
	Wooden toothpicks
	Sliced Fennel Sauce (see recipe, below)

1. Preheat oven to 350°F. In a sauté pan melt butter and 1 tablespoon of oil over medium-high heat. Add 2 teaspoons each of garlic and shallot; sauté until soft. Toss in the spinach; cook until wilted. Remove from pan to a bowl and let cool.

2. Finely chop spinach; return to bowl. Add 1 teaspoon each salt and pepper, the remaining garlic and shallot, and the Parmesan and ricotta cheeses; mix well.

3. Season chops on both sides with remaining salt and pepper; pat seasonings into meat. In a sauté pan heat ¼ cup of the oil over medium-high heat. Brown chops on both sides in hot oil until golden brown. Remove from pan. Lay chops on their bone sides and cut down the middle of the meat sides. Open chops and stuff with spinach mixture. Close chops; use toothpicks to hold sides together. Tuck spinach back in with a fork, if necessary.

4. Coat a baking sheet with the remaining 2 tablespoons olive oil. Place chops on prepared baking sheet. Bake for 25 to 30 minutes or until cooked well. Serve with Sliced Fennel Sauce.

sliced fennel sauce
makes/4 servings • serve with stuffed pork chops with ricotta and spinach

¼	cup olive oil
1	large fennel bulb, thinly sliced
1	teaspoon chopped fresh parsley
	Salt
	Black pepper
½	cup white wine
½	cup chicken stock
1	tablespoon unsalted butter
1	sprig fresh rosemary
1	sprig fresh thyme

1. In a sauté pan heat olive oil over medium-high heat.

2. Place fennel in a bowl. Add parsley and salt and pepper to taste; toss to coat. Add fennel to pan and sauté for 3 to 5 minutes or until tender. Add wine and chicken stock; cook for 5 minutes or until fennel is soft. Finish sauce by stirring in butter until melted. Garnish fennel sauce with fresh rosemary and thyme sprigs.

G's NOTES

Finishing a sauce with butter is a great way to add flavor and body.

chili-dusted pork loin
makes/6 servings

6   4-ounce pork loin medallions
1   cup all-purpose flour
½   cup chili powder
1   tablespoon garlic powder
1   tablespoon onion powder
2   teaspoons ground cumin
1   teaspoon cayenne pepper
1   teaspoon salt
1   teaspoon black pepper
1   cup buttermilk
½   cup olive oil
    Mesclun Salad with Mango
      Chutney Vinaigrette
      (see recipe, below)

1. Place pork medallions between two sheets of plastic wrap. Use a meat mallet to pound to ¼-inch thickness. Set aside.

2. In a bowl combine flour, chili powder, garlic powder, onion powder, cumin, cayenne pepper, salt, and black pepper. Place buttermilk in a separate bowl. Dip pork medallions in buttermilk, then dredge in flour mixture, coating well.

3. In a medium sauté pan heat olive oil over medium heat. Add pork medallions and sauté until well browned. Remove from pan and cut into strips. Serve on top of Mesclun Salad with Mango Chutney Vinaigrette.

mesclun salad with mango chutney vinaigrette
makes/4 to 6 servings

3   tablespoons mango chutney
2   tablespoons white wine vinegar
1   teaspoon chopped shallot
½   cup olive oil
     Salt
     Black pepper
12   ounces mesclun greens
½   pint yellow pear
       tomatoes, halved
½   pint red cherry tomatoes, halved
4   ounces Asiago cheese, shaved

1. In a food processor or blender pulse chutney until smooth. Pour chutney purée into a large bowl and whisk in white wine vinegar. Stir in shallot. Whisk in olive oil and salt and pepper to taste. (You may whisk in a tablespoon of water if dressing is too thick.)

2. Add mesclun greens to bowl with vinaigrette and toss to coat. Place greens in the middle of plate and arrange tomato halves around. If serving with Chili-Dusted Pork Loin (see recipe, above), top with pork strips. Top with shaved Asiago cheese.

veal piccata
makes/4 servings

1	pound veal loin, sliced into 4 pieces
2	teaspoons salt
2	teaspoons black pepper
½	cup all-purpose flour
9	tablespoons olive oil
1	teaspoon chopped shallot
1	teaspoon chopped garlic
¾	cup white wine
¼	cup heavy cream
2	tablespoons unsalted butter
8	kalamata olives, sliced
2	teaspoons capers
1	teaspoon lemon juice
1	teaspoon chopped Italian parsley
	Sautéed Spinach (see recipe, below)
2	French baguette slices, lightly toasted

1. Season veal on both sides with 1 teaspoon of the salt and 1 teaspoon of the pepper; pat seasonings into meat.

2. Place veal pieces between two sheets of plastic wrap. Use a mallet to pound meat to ¼-inch thickness. Dredge veal in flour to coat; pat off excess flour.

3. In a sauté pan heat 5 tablespoons of the oil over medium-high heat. Sauté veal in hot oil for 3 to 4 minutes or until golden brown on both sides, flipping veal once. Remove veal from pan and place on paper towels to absorb excess oil.

4. Add remaining 4 tablespoons oil to pan and heat over medium heat. Add shallot and garlic to pan; sauté until transparent. Carefully add wine. Simmer for 2 minutes or until liquid has reduced by half.

5. Add cream, butter, olives, capers, and the remaining 1 teaspoon salt. Stir until butter is melted. Add the remaining 1 teaspoon pepper, the lemon juice, and parsley. Reduce heat and simmer for 2 minutes. Remove from heat. Set aside and keep warm while you make Sautéed Spinach.

6. To serve, place spinach on serving plate; top with veal. Drizzle sauce from skillet over veal and spinach. Top with toasted baguette slices and garnish with additional chopped Italian parsley.

sautéed spinach
makes/4 servings

3	tablespoons olive oil
1	tablespoon unsalted butter
2	teaspoons chopped garlic
2	teaspoons chopped shallot
12	ounces fresh baby spinach

1. In a skillet heat olive oil over medium-high heat. Add butter, garlic, and shallot; cook for 1 to 2 minutes. Add spinach; toss for a minute, then remove from heat.

lamb **stroganoff**
makes/4 servings • serve with rice cakes

2   8-ounce pieces lamb loin
1   teaspoon salt
1   teaspoon black pepper
10 to 12 button mushrooms
3   tablespoons olive oil
1   teaspoon chopped shallot
1   teaspoon chopped garlic
1   medium onion, diced
1   small green bell pepper,
       seeded and sliced
1   small orange bell pepper,
       seeded and sliced
1   small red bell pepper,
       seeded and sliced
¼   cup white wine
¼   cup heavy cream
¼   cup beef stock
¼   cup chicken stock
2   tablespoons unsalted butter
2   tablespoons sour cream
    Rice Cakes (see recipe, opposite)

1. Season lamb on all sides with salt and black pepper. Cut lamb pieces in half, then cut into small squares; set aside. Cut mushrooms into quarters; set aside.

2. In a sauté pan heat 2 tablespoons of the olive oil over medium-high heat. Add shallot and garlic; sauté for 1 minute. Add lamb, mushrooms, and the remaining 1 tablespoon olive oil; mix well. Add onion and sliced bell pepper; sauté until vegetables are just tender and lamb is browned.

3. Add wine, cream, beef stock, and chicken stock; mix well. Bring to a boil; simmer until lamb is cooked well. Stir in butter and sour cream. Serve with Rice Cakes.

G's NOTES
This may also be served with your favorite egg noodle or butter noodle recipe.

rice cakes
makes/4 servings

1 cup cooked short grain
    white rice
1 cup cooked brown rice
2 eggs
½ cup chopped fresh chives
5 tablespoons all-purpose flour
¼ cup shredded Parmesan cheese
2 teaspoons salt
2 teaspoons black pepper
¾ cup canola oil

1. Place white and brown rice in a bowl. Add eggs, chives, flour, Parmesan cheese, salt, and pepper; mix well.

2. Take a 3-inch ring mold* and put it on a flat plate. Fill the mold with rice mixture, patting it down with a spoon to secure the shape.

3. Add canola oil to a sauté pan and preheat over medium-high heat. Remove ring from rice cake and with a spatula place rice cake into sauté pan. Sauté on both sides until lightly brown and stiff. Remove rice cake from pan and let drain on paper towels. Repeat with remaining rice mixture.

* Lightly grease the inside of the ring mold with oil to make it easy to remove the rice cakes.

 G's NOTES
This side dish may be used with Lamb Stroganoff (see recipe, opposite) or with other dishes you may put together.

sautéed salmon and shrimp with brie
makes/4 servings

4   4-ounce pieces salmon fillet, skin removed
8   ounces medium shrimp, peeled and butterflied
1   tablespoon lemon-pepper seasoning
¼   cup olive oil
4   ounces Brie cheese, cut into 8 slices
2   tablespoons unsalted butter
1   tablespoon chopped garlic
1   tablespoon chopped shallot
½   cup white wine
1   lemon, juiced
1   teaspoon salt
1   teaspoon black pepper

1. Preheat oven to 375°F. Season salmon and shrimp with lemon-pepper seasoning. Set shrimp aside.

2. In a large sauté pan heat olive oil over medium heat. Add salmon and sauté for 3 minutes per side or until golden brown. Remove salmon from pan and place on a baking sheet. Bake for 8 to 12 minutes or until salmon is three-quarters of the way done. In the last 2 minutes of baking, place 2 slices of Brie on each fillet.

3. Meanwhile, in a medium sauté pan melt 1 tablespoon of the butter over medium heat. Add garlic and shallot; sauté for 2 minutes. Add shrimp; cook for 2 minutes more. Add white wine, lemon juice, salt, and black pepper. Finish sauce by stirring in the remaining 1 tablespoon butter until melted.

4. When salmon is done, place it on a plate. Pour shrimp and sauce over top.

G's NOTES
To butterfly means to split the shrimp open but not in half.

blackened whitefish **piccata** with arugula
makes/4 servings

4	6-ounce whitefish fillets, skin on
¼	cup Blackening Spice (see recipe, below)
¼	cup olive oil
2	tablespoons unsalted butter
2	tablespoons chopped garlic
2	tablespoons chopped shallot
2	tablespoons capers
½	cup white wine
¼	cup chicken stock
1	tablespoon lemon juice
10	pitted kalamata olives, slivered
	Salt
	Black pepper
6	ounces fresh arugula

1. Sprinkle Blackening Spice on meat sides of fish until well coated. In a medium sauté pan heat olive oil over medium heat. Place fish in pan, skin sides down; cook until skin is crispy. Turn fillets over.

2. Add 1 tablespoon of the butter, the garlic, shallot, and capers to pan; sauté until tender. Add wine, chicken stock, lemon juice, olives, and salt and pepper to taste. Simmer for 5 to 7 minutes or until sauce is desired consistency. Finish the sauce by stirring in the remaining 1 tablespoon butter until melted.

3. To serve, place fish on serving plates. Pour pan sauce over fish and garnish with arugula.

blackening spice
makes/about ⅔ cup

2	tablespoons red pepper flakes
2	tablespoons garlic powder
2	tablespoons onion powder
2	tablespoons dark chili powder
1	tablespoon paprika
1	tablespoon salt
1	teaspoon dried parsley
1	teaspoon dried thyme
1	teaspoon celery powder
	Pinch cayenne pepper

1. In a bowl stir together all ingredients. Store in an airtight container

walnut-encrusted grouper

makes/4 servings

¼   cup unsalted butter
½   cup packed brown sugar
1   pound walnuts
1   cup panko bread crumbs*
¼   cup heavy cream
1   egg yolk
2   tablespoons olive oil
4   6-ounce pieces grouper,
     skin removed
     Salt
     Black pepper

1. Line a baking sheet with parchment paper; set aside. In a medium saucepan heat butter and brown sugar over medium heat until sugar is dissolved. (It should be a little thick.) Add the walnuts and mix well. Using an oven mitt, pour walnut mixture onto prepared baking sheet; spread out on pan to cool.** (Mixture should harden like peanut brittle.)

2. When walnut mixture is cool, break it into pieces and place pieces in a food processor; finely chop. Pour mixture into a large bowl and stir in the bread crumbs. Set aside.

3. In a small bowl whisk cream and egg yolk together; set aside. In a large skillet heat the olive oil over medium heat. Dip one side of the fish into the egg mixture and place on a plate. Sprinkle salt and pepper on the side that has been coated with the egg mixture. Next dip the side of the fish with the egg mixture into the walnut mixture, patting so mixture will stick.

4. Place fish in the hot skillet, coated side down. Cook for 3 to 4 minutes or until coated side is brown. Turn fish over and cook for 3 to 4 minutes more. Repeat rocedure with all fish, adding extra olive oil to pan if needed. Serve with Asparagus and Carrot Medley (see recipe, opposite) and Ginger Potatoes (see recipe, opposite).

* Panko bread crumbs are used in Japanese cooking for coating fried foods. They are coarser than typical dried bread crumbs and make a very crunchy coating.

** Never taste or touch hot sugar; serious burns may occur.

asparagus and carrot medley
makes/4 servings

8   ounces asparagus, cut into
      2-inch lengths
8   ounces baby carrots
2   tablespoons olive oil
2   tablespoons chopped garlic
2   tablespoons chopped shallot
¼   cup white wine
2   tablespoons unsalted butter
      Salt
      Black pepper

1. In a large pot bring 3 quarts water to a boil. Add asparagus and boil for 2 minutes. Remove asparagus from water; set aside. Add carrots to water; boil for 2 to 3 minutes or just until tender. Remove from water; set aside.

2. In a large skillet heat olive oil over medium heat. Add garlic and shallot; mix well. Add the asparagus and carrots and the wine; simmer until wine is reduced by half. Stir in butter until melted. Season to taste with salt and pepper.

ginger potatoes
makes/4 to 6 servings

3   large potatoes, peeled and cubed
2   tablespoons olive oil
2   tablespoons chopped garlic
2   tablespoons chopped shallot
3   tablespoons unsalted butter
      Salt
      Black pepper
2   tablespoons minced fresh ginger
2   tablespoons chopped
      fresh parsley
¼   cup diced yellow tomato

1. In a large pot bring 3 quarts water to a boil. Add potato to water and boil for 3 minutes or until cubes are are just tender but not mushy. Drain the potato cubes; set aside.

2. In a large sauté pan heat olive oil over medium heat. Add garlic and shallot. Add butter and stir until melted. Add potato cubes to pan, stirring to coat. Season to taste with salt and pepper. Add ginger and parsley; mix well. Stir in tomato.

maryland **crab cakes**
makes/12 crab cakes

1   **pound lump crabmeat**
3   **tablespoons Dijon mustard**
3   **tablespoons Worcestershire sauce**
2   **tablespoons mayonnaise**
2   **tablespoons hot sauce**
2   **teaspoons chopped fresh parsley**
2   **teaspoons Old Bay® seasoning**
1   **teaspoon cracked white pepper**
1   **teaspoon black pepper**
3   **tablespoons olive oil**
3   **tablespoons diced red bell pepper**
3   **tablespoons diced green bell pepper**
1   **cup regular bread crumbs**
1   **egg**
1   **cup panko bread crumbs***
    Dijon mustard

1. In a large mixing bowl stir together crabmeat, mustard, Worcestershire sauce, mayonnaise, hot sauce, parsley, Old Bay seasoning, white pepper, and black pepper. Set aside.

2. In a small frying pan heat $1\frac{1}{2}$ tablespoons of the olive oil over medium heat. Add red and green bell pepper; cook until it is wilted. Set aside to cool.

3. When bell pepper is cool, add to bowl with crabmeat along with $\frac{1}{4}$ cup regular bread crumbs. Stir together. Add egg to crab mixture and combine well. In a shallow dish combine remaining regular bread crumbs and panko bread crumbs.

4. Take $\frac{1}{12}$ of the crab mixture and coat it with bread crumbs. Shape into a round cake. Repeat with remaining crab mixture and bread crumbs.

5. Heat the remaining $1\frac{1}{2}$ tablespoons olive oil in a skillet over medium-high heat. Fry crab cakes until golden brown on each side. Serve crab cakes with a touch of Dijon mustard.

* Panko bread crumbs are used in Japanese cooking for coating fried foods. They are coarser than typical dried bread crumbs and make a very crunchy coating.

G's NOTES
The crab cakes also taste great when served with Basil Mayonnaise (see recipe, page 230).

tuna and crab salad sandwiches

makes/2 servings • see photo, below and on page 176

2　6-ounce pieces seared tuna loin
½　cup crabmeat
1　stalk celery, chopped
½　cup chopped red onion
2　tablespoons chopped fresh
　　Italian parsley
2　tablespoons capers
6　hard-boiled egg whites, chopped
3　tablespoons mayonnaise
3　tablespoons Dijon mustard
1　teaspoon salt
1　teaspoon black pepper
4　slices sourdough bread
4　slices Gruyère cheese
⅓　cup unsalted butter
1　6-ounce bag favorite potato
　　chips (optional)

1. Crumble seared tuna and place in a bowl with crabmeat. Stir in celery, red onion, parsley, and capers. Add egg white, mayonnaise, mustard, salt, and pepper; mix gently.

2. Spread tuna mixture evenly on two slices of bread. Top with Gruyère cheese and remaining bread slices.

3. In a skillet melt butter over medium heat. Add sandwiches to skillet and cook until toasted on both sides. If desired, serve with potato chips.

fettuccine with shrimp and
oven-roasted tomatoes in a light cream sauce

makes/4 servings

5	plum tomatoes
10	tablespoons olive oil
6	teaspoons kosher salt
3	tablespoons balsamic vinegar
3	teaspoons black pepper
2	teaspoons chopped fresh thyme
2	teaspoons chopped fresh parsley
2	teaspoons chopped fresh rosemary
2	teaspoons chopped fresh oregano
2	tablespoons chopped garlic
2	tablespoons chopped shallot
1	cup vegetable stock
1	cup heavy cream
½	cup white wine
12	ounces fettuccine
20	medium shrimp, peeled and deveined
¼	cup grated Parmesan cheese

1. Preheat oven to 375°F. Cut tomatoes in half and place in a bowl. Add 2 tablespoons of the olive oil, 2 teaspoons of the kosher salt, the balsamic vinegar, 1 teaspoon of the pepper, and 1 teaspoon each of the thyme, parsley, rosemary, and oregano; mix well. Line a baking sheet with parchment paper; coat with 2 tablespoons of the olive oil. Lay tomatoes on baking sheet and roast for 20 to 30 minutes or until tomatoes lose most of their liquid. Set aside.

2. In a medium sauté pan heat 2 tablespoons of the olive oil over medium heat. Add garlic and shallot; sauté for 1 to 2 minutes. Add 2 tablespoons of the olive oil, the vegetable stock, cream, and white wine; mix well. Season with 2 teaspoons of the salt and the remaining 2 teaspoons pepper; stir sauce.

3. Bring a pot of water to a boil. Add 2 tablespoons of the olive oil and the remaining 2 teaspoons salt. Add fettuccine and boil for 4 to 6 minutes or until just tender.

4. Season shrimp to taste with additional salt and pepper. In a large skillet heat the remaining 2 tablespoons olive oil over medium-high heat. Add shrimp and sauté about 2 minutes or until pink and firm; set skillet aside.

5. Add Parmesan cheese to sauce, then add the remaining 1 teaspoon each thyme, parsley, rosemary, and oregano; mix well.

6. Drain pasta and add to skillet with shrimp; toss to combine. Add sauce to skillet and let simmer for 1 to 2 minutes.

7. Add four of the oven-roasted tomatoes to the pasta; mix well. Place pasta in a large serving bowl. Chop remaining tomato and use it to garnish pasta.

coconut shrimp
makes/4 servings

1   pound medium shrimp
¼   cup lemon juice
2   tablespoons ground ginger
2   tablespoons curry powder
2   tablespoons garlic powder
1   tablespoon ground allspice
    Pinch cayenne pepper
2   cups all-purpose flour
½   cup skim milk
½   cup coconut cream
2   tablespoons baking powder
2   tablespoons honey
1   cup sweet shredded coconut
1   cup regular shredded coconut
2   cups peanut oil
1   cup bread crumbs

1. Peel and devein shrimp; place in a bowl. Add lemon juice, ginger, curry powder, garlic powder, allspice, and cayenne pepper; mix well.

2. In a large bowl combine 1 cup of the flour, the milk, coconut cream, baking powder, and honey. Mix until batter is smooth. Stir in ¼ cup each of the sweet and regular shredded coconut.

3. In a deep frying pan or deep-fryer heat peanut oil over medium heat. Place the remaining 1 cup flour on a large plate. In a bowl stir together the remaining coconut and the bread crumbs.

4. Dip shrimp in the flour, shaking off excess. Next dip the shrimp in the batter. Finally coat the shrimp with the coconut mixture. Place coated shrimp in hot oil and cook for 5 to 6 minutes or until shrimp is golden brown. Place shrimp on paper towels to absorb excess oil. Repeat with remaining shrimp. Serve hot.

shrimp and scallops **scampi**

makes/6 to 8 servings

1	**pound medium shrimp, peeled and deveined**
1	**pound bay scallops**
	Salt
	Lemon-pepper seasoning
¼	**cup olive oil**
3	**tablespoons chopped garlic**
3	**tablespoons chopped shallot**
¼	**cup unsalted butter**
½	**cup chicken stock**
1	**cup white wine**
1	**lemon, juiced**
½	**cup heavy cream**
2	**tablespoons chopped fresh parsley**
	Confetti Rice (see recipe, opposite)

1. Season the shrimp and scallops with salt and lemon-pepper seasoning. In a large skillet heat olive oil over medium-high heat. Add shrimp and scallops; sauté for a few minutes or until both are firm and flesh is opaque. Remove from pan and set aside.

2. In the same skillet sauté the garlic and shallot over medium-high heat for 1 minute. Stir in the butter until melted. Slowly stir in the chicken stock. Add white wine and lemon juice. Bring to a boil; reduce heat. Simmer until reduced by half.

3. Slowly stir in cream. Return shrimp and scallops to pan along with 1 tablespoon of the parsley. Serve over Confetti Rice. Garnish with the remaining parsley.

confetti rice
makes/8 servings

1	tablespoon olive oil
2	cups uncooked rice
¼	cup chopped red bell pepper
¼	cup chopped green bell pepper
¼	cup chopped yellow bell pepper
2	tablespoons chopped garlic
2	tablespoons chopped shallot
3	cups chicken stock
¼	cup chopped carrot
1	tablespoon unsalted butter
1	teaspoon garlic salt
1	teaspoon lemon-pepper
	seasoning
	Pinch saffron
¼	cup chopped scallion

1. In a large sauté pan heat olive oil over medium-high heat. Add rice, bell pepper, garlic, and shallot; cook for 1 to 2 minutes or until rice is coated well. Stir in chicken stock. Stir in carrot. Add butter, garlic salt, lemon-pepper seasoning, and saffron; mix well.

2. Bring to a boil; reduce heat. Cover and simmer for 10 minutes or until rice is nearly done. Stir in scallion.

spinach, mushroom, and goat cheese ravioli

makes/4 servings

3   tablespoons + 1 teaspoon
    olive oil
½   cup sliced shiitake mushrooms
    Salt
    Black pepper
8   ounces fresh baby spinach
4   tablespoons goat
    cheese (chèvre)
1   tablespoon chopped garlic
1   tablespoon chopped shallot
1   large egg
¼   cup heavy cream
12 wonton wrappers
1   cup cornstarch
2   teaspoons unsalted butter
    Plum Tomato Filetto Sauce
    (see recipe, opposite)

1. In a skillet heat 2 tablespoons of the olive oil over medium heat. Add mushrooms and salt and pepper to taste; sauté for 3 to 4 minutes or until mushrooms are tender. Place mushrooms in a food processor. Process until finely chopped. Set aside to cool.

2. In the same skillet sauté the baby spinach for about 1 minute or until wilted. Cool slightly and process in a food processor until finely chopped.

3. In a bowl combine mushrooms, spinach, 3 tablespoons of the goat cheese, the garlic, shallot, and the 1 teaspoon olive oil; mix well. Set filling aside. In a small bowl beat egg and cream together until smooth.

4. Using a pastry brush, brush egg mixture onto a wonton wrapper. (Note: Place unused wonton wrappers between damp paper towels to keep them from drying out.) Spoon about a teaspoon of the filling in center of wrapper. Fold wonton into desired shape (triangle or rectangle), pressing edges with fingertips to seal. Repeat with remaining wonton wrappers and filling. Dredge ravioli lightly in cornstarch.

5. Bring a pot of water to boil over high heat. Add the remaining 1 tablespoon olive oil and a pinch of salt. Add ravioli to water and cook about 3 minutes or until they float and are tender but not mushy.

6. With a slotted spoon gently remove ravioli and place in a sauté pan. Add butter to pan and stir over medium heat. When butter is melted, remove ravioli and place on plate; pour pan drippings over top. Serve Plum Tomato Filetto Sauce over ravioli. Top with remaining 1 tablespoon goat cheese and a pinch of pepper.

G's NOTES

Be sure to make all of your ravioli at one time and place on the side. If water is boiling too rapidly, turn down slightly. You don't want a hard boil that may break your ravioli.

plum tomato filetto sauce

makes/about 2 cups • serve over spinach, mushroom, and goat cheese ravioli

¼   cup olive oil
1   tablespoon chopped garlic
1   tablespoon chopped shallot
4   ounces bacon, diced
3   plum tomatoes, diced
2   pieces canned plum
      tomatoes, crushed
1   tablespoon chopped fresh basil
¼   cup white wine
1   tablespoon chopped fresh
      Italian parsley
1   teaspoon salt
1   teaspoon black pepper
½   cup heavy cream
3   tablespoons unsalted butter

1. In a sauté pan heat olive oil over medium heat. Add garlic and shallot; sauté for 2 minutes. Add diced bacon and cook until crispy. Stir in all tomatoes. Add basil followed by the white wine; stir. Season with parsley, salt, and pepper.

2. Stir in cream and simmer for 5 to 7 minutes or until slightly thickened. Finish by stirring in butter until melted.

building a great dish

{ Experience flavor excitement in every bite with G. Garvin's richly seasoned dishes. }

When cooking, everything must have its own identity. By this I mean that each dish is like a great song or a well-dressed woman. A great song has melody, chords, and strings, bass, and drums, followed by wonderful lyrics and a fantastic vocalist; together you've got one great song. (Mario: You Should Let Me Love You.) Now, as far as a well-dressed woman ... Each layer of clothing has its own identity. A wonderful skirt flows to her ankles. A simple sleeveless shirt wraps her upper body. She then ties a beautiful shoulder shirt around her waist and maybe adds a shawl. Finish off with an open-toe Jimmy Choo, a scarf in her hair, and gorgeous jewelry. When she enters the room, it's simple but beautiful. In the same way, you build a great dish from the bottom up. Every ingredient has its own identity and comes together for one amazing experience.

herb and black pepper-crusted tuna tataki
with wasabi cream sauce

makes/4 servings

4 ounces wasabi powder
¼ cup water
2 tablespoons sour cream*
2 8-ounce pieces tuna loin
4 tablespoons olive oil
2 tablespoons chopped
   fresh rosemary
2 tablespoons chopped
   fresh thyme
2 tablespoons chopped fresh mint
2 tablespoons chopped
   fresh chives
1 teaspoon salt
¼ cup coarsely ground
   black pepper
12 ounces frisée
8 pieces long chives
   Fresh Italian parsley

1. For wasabi cream sauce, put wasabi powder in a bowl. Slowly stir in the water to create a paste. Add the sour cream and mix well. (The sauce should have the consistency of a very thin mayonnaise.) Set aside.

2. Coat the tuna with 2 tablespoons of the olive oil. Season with rosemary, thyme, mint, chopped chives, and salt. Season with pepper and pat down to make sure herbs and pepper stick to tuna.

3. Place a sauté pan over medium-high heat and coat with the remaining 2 tablespoons olive oil. Place tuna in hot pan and sear for about a minute. Turn tuna over and sear on the other side for about a minute. (Be sure not to overcook the tuna.) Remove tuna from the pan; set aside and let tuna rest for 1 to 2 minutes.

4. Cut tuna into ½-inch slices and fan out. Drizzle wasabi cream on plates. Place sliced tuna on the plates on top of the cream. Place the frisée behind the tuna. Garnish with long chives and Italian parsley.

* The more sour cream you add to the wasabi paste, the milder it will be.

sautéed pork medallions with dried
apricot, granny smith apple, and raisin compote

makes/4 servings

3	tablespoons olive oil
1	pound pork tenderloin, cut into 8 medallions
	Seasoned salt
	All-purpose flour
2	tablespoons unsalted butter
1	tablespoon chopped shallot
6	dried apricot halves, diced and soaked*
2	tablespoons raisins, soaked*
½	cup diced Granny Smith apple
¼	cup apple cider
¼	cup chicken stock
	Pinch ground cinnamon
	Kosher salt
	Black pepper
	Mashed Sweet Potatoes (see recipe, opposite)
	Haricots Verts (see recipe, opposite)

1. In a sauté pan heat olive oil over medium heat. Season pork medallions with seasoned salt. Dredge medallions in flour to coat; shake off excess flour. Sauté medallions in hot oil for 5 to 7 minutes or until golden on both sides. Remove from pan and set aside.

2. For compote, melt 1 tablespoon of the butter in pan. Add shallot and sauté for 2 minutes. Add drained apricots and raisins and the apple; sauté for 2 minutes. Add apple cider, chicken stock, and cinnamon. Simmer until reduced by half. Finish compote by whisking in the remaining 1 tablespoon butter.

3. Return pork medallions to pan and simmer for 1 minute to heat through. Season to taste with salt and pepper.

4. To serve, place Mashed Sweet Potatoes in center of plate and place Haricots Verts around the side. Top sweet potatoes with pork medallions, then compote.

* Soak diced dried apricots and raisins in ½ cup hot water for 10 minutes. Drain.

mashed sweet potatoes

makes/4 servings

3   medium sweet potatoes
¼   cup milk
¼   cup heavy cream
2   tablespoons unsalted butter
1   tablespoon packed brown sugar
     Pinch ground cinnamon
     Pinch ground nutmeg
     Pinch salt

1. In a pot of boiling water cook sweet potatoes with their skins on until tender. Cool and peel. Dice sweet potatoes and place in a saucepan. Add milk, cream, butter, brown sugar, cinnamon, nutmeg, and salt. Heat through, stirring frequently. Mash to desired consistency.

haricots verts tied with chives

makes/4 servings • see photo/page 178

     Salt
     Black pepper
1   pound haricots verts (French
     green beans), washed
1   bunch fresh chives, 5 to 6
     inches long
1   tablespoon olive oil
1   tablespoon chopped garlic
1   tablespoon chopped shallot
1½   teaspoons unsalted butter

1. Bring a pot of water with a pinch each of salt and pepper to boiling. Add haricots verts and boil for 3 to 5 minutes or until bright green. Remove haricots verts from pot and place in ice water. Drain and pat dry.

2. In the same pot of water, blanch chives for 1 to 2 seconds. Remove chives from pot and place in ice water also. Drain. Bundle up haricots verts in groups of 5 and tie bundles with chives

3. In a medium sauté pan heat olive oil over medium heat. Add garlic and shallot; sauté for 2 minutes. Add haricots verts bundles; season to taste with salt and pepper. Sauté until heated through. Add butter and stir until melted. Serve haricots verts as a side dish.

G's NOTES

Haricots verts is the French term for green string beans.

grilled **pork tenderloin** with port wine demi-glace
makes/4 servings

8   pork tenderloin medallions,
      ½ inch thick
3   tablespoons olive oil
    Salt
    Black pepper
2   tablespoons unsalted butter
1   tablespoon chopped garlic
1   tablespoon chopped shallot
1   cup veal stock
½   cup port wine
1   teaspoon chopped fresh
      rosemary
1   teaspoon chopped fresh thyme
    Fried Risotto Cakes (see recipe,
      opposite)

1. Preheat oven to 350°F. Coat pork with 2 tablespoons of the oil. Season with salt and pepper. Heat a grill pan over medium-high heat. Grill pork for 4 to 7 minutes per side or until browned. Place in hot oven to finish pork to desired doneness.

2. For demi-glace, in a medium sauté pan heat the remaining 1 tablespoon olive oil and 1 tablespoon of the butter over medium heat. Add garlic and shallot; sauté until soft. Add veal stock, port wine, rosemary, and thyme. Simmer until reduced by half. Finish by stirring in the remaining 1 tablespoon butter until melted. Add pork medallions to sauce.

3. To serve, place Fried Risotto Cakes on plates and top with pork medallions and demi-glace.

fried **risotto cakes**
makes/4 to 6 servings

4½ cups chicken stock
¼ cup unsalted butter
1 medium onion, chopped
1½ cups Arborio rice
1 cup white wine
½ cup grated Parmesan cheese
½ cup chopped scallion
2 tablespoons olive oil
½ cup all-purpose flour

1. In a large saucepan bring the chicken stock to a simmer. In a medium saucepan melt butter over medium heat. Add the onion and sauté for 5 minutes or until soft. Add the rice and stir until coated.

2. Increase the heat to medium-high. Add the wine. Cook, stirring constantly, for 4 minutes or until wine is absorbed. Add about 1 cup chicken stock (enough to just cover the rice) and cook, stirring constantly, until the stock is absorbed. Continue adding stock, 1 cup at a time, stirring until it is absorbed before adding more. The rice is done when it is just cooked through and lightly bound with a creamy liquid after about 15 minutes.

3. Remove risotto from heat and stir in Parmesan cheese and scallion. Spread risotto evenly in a greased sheet pan and refrigerate until very firm, at least 4 hours or overnight

4. In a large sauté pan heat the olive oil over medium heat. Form risotto cakes by shaping handfuls of risotto into 3x½-inch disks. Dredge the cakes in flour to coat. Sauté cakes in hot oil until golden.

158

roasted short ribs

makes/4 servings

- 2 pounds boneless beef short ribs
- 1 tablespoon kosher salt
- 1 tablespoon garlic salt
- 1 tablespoon onion powder
- 1 tablespoon seasoned salt
- 1 tablespoon finely ground black pepper
- 1 cup all-purpose flour
- ¼ cup + dash olive oil
- 2 large onions, diced
- ¼ cup chopped garlic
- ¼ cup chopped shallot
- 3 sprigs rosemary
- 2 cups white wine
- 2 cups chicken stock
- 1 cup water
  Goat Cheese Potatoes (see recipe, opposite)
  String Beans (see recipe, right)

1. Preheat oven to 350°F. Trim fat from short ribs and rinse ribs with cool water. Season ribs with kosher salt, garlic salt, onion powder, seasoned salt, and pepper. Pat the seasonings in so they stick to the ribs. Set aside. Place flour on a large plate; set aside.

2. In a large roasting pan heat ¼ cup of the olive oil over medium heat. Dip both sides of a short rib into the flour. Place rib in hot pan. Repeat until all ribs are floured and are in pan. Cook until ribs are golden and turn ribs over.

3. Add the onion, garlic, and shallot to pan and mix well. Add the rosemary and a dash of olive oil; mix well again. Add white wine, chicken stock, and water. Bring to a simmer.

4. Place a piece of foil over the roasting pan. Place pan in the oven and roast for 1½ to 2 hours or until ribs are tender, adding more liquid as needed.

5. To serve, place Goat Cheese Potatoes on a serving plate. Top with ribs. Arrange String Beans around side of the plate. Spoon pan gravy over ribs and potatoes.

string beans: In a large pot bring 3 quarts of water to a boil. Add 8 ounces green string beans and boil for 3 minutes. Remove beans from pot and place in ice water; drain. In a large skillet heat 2 tablespoons olive oil over medium heat. Add 3 tablespoons chopped garlic, 2 tablespoons chopped shallot, and 2 tablespoons unsalted butter; sauté for 2 minutes. Add the green beans; stir to combine. Season to taste with salt and pepper.

goat cheese potatoes
makes/4 to 6 servings

3 large potatoes, cubed
½ cup milk
½ cup heavy cream
2 tablespoons unsalted butter
4 ounces goat cheese (chèvre)
Salt
Black pepper

1. In a 6-quart pot place potatoes and enough water to cover. Bring to a boil. Boil until potatoes are tender. Drain potatoes; return to pot. Place over very low heat. Add milk and cream. Using a whisk or potato masher, mash potatoes. (If necessary, add more cream to make potatoes desired consistency.)

2. Add butter and mix well. Add goat cheese and mix until evenly blended. Season to taste with salt and pepper.

blackened **veal chops**

makes/4 servings

¼ cup olive oil
4 8-ounce veal chops
¼ cup Blackening Spice (see recipe, page 139)
2 tablespoons unsalted butter
2 teaspoons chopped garlic
2 teaspoons chopped shallot
6 morel mushrooms, halved
  Salt
  Black pepper
  Oven-Roasted Tomatoes and White Bean Ragoût (see recipe, opposite)

1. On a griddle heat olive oil over medium-high heat. Season veal chops on both sides with Blackening Spice. Pat seasonings into meat. Cook chops on hot griddle until both sides are brown; set aside.

2. In a sauté pan melt butter over medium heat. Add garlic and shallot; sauté for 2 minutes. Stir in mushrooms; sauté briefly. Season to taste with salt and pepper.

3. To serve, place White Bean Ragoût in center of a serving dish. Top with veal chops. Top chops with Oven-Roasted Tomatoes and the sautéed mushrooms.

oven-roasted tomatoes and **white bean ragoût**

makes/4 servings

2	whole plum tomatoes, cored and halved lengthwise
3	tablespoons chopped garlic
3	tablespoons chopped shallot
1	tablespoon chopped fresh parsley
7	tablespoons olive oil
1	tablespoon balsamic vinegar
1	cup canned cannellini beans
½	cup diced celery, blanched
4	small potatoes, peeled and cooked
½	cup heavy cream
1	teaspoon salt
1	teaspoon black pepper
4	ounces fresh baby spinach
1	tablespoon unsalted butter

1. Preheat oven to 375°F. For oven-roasted tomatoes, in a small roasting pan place tomatoes, cut sides up. Sprinkle 2 tablespoons of the garlic, 2 tablespoons of the shallot, and the parsley over tomatoes. Drizzle 5 tablespoons of the oil and the balsamic vinegar over top. Roast for 20 to 30 minutes or until tomatoes have lost most of their liquid.

2. For ragout, heat remaining 2 tablespoons olive oil in a small pot over medium-high heat Add remaining 1 tablespoon garlic, 1 tablespoon shallot, the beans, and celery. Cube potatoes, then add to pot. Add cream, salt, and pepper; reduce heat and heat through. Stir spinach into pot. Stir in butter to finish.

grilled lamb

makes/4 servings

2   8-ounce pieces lamb loin
¼   cup olive oil
2   teaspoons salt
1   teaspoon black pepper
    Candied Sweet Potato and Yam
      (see recipe, opposite)
    Mushroom and Goat Cheese
      Crumble (see recipe, opposite)
    Candied lemon and orange zest*

1. Coat lamb loin with the oil. Season lamb on all sides with salt and pepper. Heat a grill pan over medium-high heat. Grill lamb on all sides until desired doneness (145°F for medium rare).

2. Slice lamb diagonally into thin slices. Place sliced lamb on top of Candied Sweet Potato and Yam. Spoon Mushroom and Goat Cheese Crumble on top of lamb. Garnish with candied lemon and orange zest.

* To candy lemon and orange zest, place zest of 1 lemon and 1 orange in a sauté pan with 2 tablespoons of sugar and 2 tablespoons water. Heat until sugar is dissolved and mixture starts to bubble. Remove zest from pan and place on a paper towel to cool.

candied **sweet potato** and yam

1	medium yam
1	medium sweet potato
2	tablespoons olive oil
2	tablespoons unsalted butter
3	tablespoons packed brown sugar
	Pinch ground cinnamon
	Pinch ground allspice
	Pinch ground nutmeg
	Pinch black pepper

1. In a pot of boiling water cook yam and sweet potato with their skin on until tender. Cool, peel, and dice, then set aside. (You should have 1 cup of each.)

2. In a sauté pan heat olive oil over medium-high heat. Add the butter and let melt. Add yam, sweet potato, brown sugar, and spices. Reduce heat; let simmer until sugar is melted and yam and sweet potato are glazed. Spoon yam and sweet potato mixture into serving dish.

G's NOTES

Boiling sweet potatoes and yams with the skin on allows their meat to retain its flavor.

mushroom and **goat cheese crumble**

½	cup mushrooms, sautéed
4	ounces goat cheese (chèvre), crumbled
3	tablespoons olive oil
	Pinch salt
	Pinch black pepper

1. In a bowl stir together all ingredients.

rack of lamb with potatoes, carrots, and asparagus

makes/4 to 6 servings

1   1½- to 2-pound rack of lamb
1   teaspoon salt
1   teaspoon black pepper
3   tablespoons olive oil
    Dry Rub Blend (see recipe, right)
2   tablespoons dry bread crumbs
    Red Potatoes (see recipe,
      opposite)
    Carrots and Asparagus (see
      recipe, opposite)
    Balsamic vinegar
    Freshly ground black pepper

1. Preheat oven to 350°F. Season rack of lamb with salt and pepper. In an oven-safe sauté pan heat olive oil over medium heat. Sear lamb in pan until golden brown on all sides. Remove from heat.

2. Spread Dry Rub Blend over browned lamb with a spoon. Roast for 35 to 40 minutes or until the internal temperature registers 150°F for medium (160°F for well done). In the last 15 minutes of roasting, sprinkle bread crumbs over lamb.

3. To serve, put Red Potatoes on a platter. Add Carrots and Asparagus to the dish. Slice lamb and place on top of vegetables. To finish, drizzle with additional olive oil and a touch of balsamic vinegar. Top with freshly ground black pepper to make the dish complete.

dry rub blend: In a bowl combine ¼ cup Dijon mustard, 3 tablespoons olive oil, 1 tablespoon chopped shallot, 1 tablespoon chopped garlic, 1 teaspoon chopped fresh parsley, a pinch salt, a pinch black pepper, and a pinch cracked white pepper.

red **potatoes**
makes/4 to 6 servings

5	small red potatoes, quartered
1	tablespoon chopped garlic
1	tablespoon chopped shallot
1	tablespoon chopped fresh rosemary
1	tablespoon chopped fresh thyme
2	tablespoons unsalted butter

1. Preheat oven to 350°F. Place potato quarters in a baking dish. Add garlic, shallot, rosemary, and thyme. Dot quarters with butter. Roast in oven for 20 to 30 minutes or until potato quarters are tender.

carrots and asparagus
makes/4 to 6 servings

3	tablespoons salt
2	tablespoons black pepper
1	bunch pencil thin asparagus
12	baby carrots
2	tablespoons olive oil
1	teaspoon chopped shallot
1	teaspoon chopped garlic
1	teaspoon butter
	Salt
	Black pepper

1. Fill a large pot halfway with water; bring to a boil with salt and pepper. Place asparagus in pot; boil for 3 minutes. Remove asparagus and place in ice water. Place baby carrots in pot; boil for 4 minutes. Remove and place in ice water. Drain vegetables well.

2. In a sauté pan heat olive oil over medium heat. Add shallot, garlic, and butter. Stir until butter is melted. Add the carrots and asparagus; sauté for 1 to 2 minutes to heat through. Season with salt and pepper.

grilled mahi mahi

makes/4 servings

4   8-ounce pieces mahi mahi
     Kosher salt
     Black pepper
     Leek and Asparagus Ragoût
       (see recipe, opposite)
     Pineapple, Mango, and Tomato
       Salsa (see recipe, opposite)

1. Heat grill pan over medium heat. Season mahi mahi with salt and pepper. Grill for 4 minutes per side or until fish is opaque and flakes easily.

2. To serve, place fish on bed of Leek and Asparagus Ragoût and top with Pineapple, Mango, and Tomato Salsa.

leek and asparagus ragoût
makes/4 servings

1 pound asparagus
2 leeks, cleaned*
1 tablespoon olive oil
1 tablespoon unsalted butter
1 tablespoon chopped garlic
1 tablespoon chopped shallot
1 teaspoon chopped fresh
   rosemary
1 teaspoon chopped fresh thyme
   Salt
   Black pepper

1. In a large pot bring 2 quarts of water to a boil. Cut ½ inch off of the bottom of asparagus stems.** Place the asparagus in the boiling water for 5 minutes, then transfer to ice water. (Note: Leave the water boiling for the leeks.) Once the asparagus is cool, drain it, dice it, and set it aside. Repeat with leeks.

2. In a sauté pan heat olive oil and butter over medium heat. Add garlic and shallot; sauté for 2 minutes. Add leeks, asparagus, rosemary, thyme, salt, and pepper; stir to combine and heat through.

* To clean leeks, fill a large bowl with water and trim the green tops off of the leeks. Cut leeks in half lengthwise, separate leaves, and place them in the water. Make sure they float to ensure any sand falls to the bottom of the bowl. Remove leeks by gently lifting them out of the water, leaving sand and dirt on the bottom of the bowl.

** Leave the rubber band around asparagus bunch to make it easier to retrieve it from the water.

pineapple, mango, and tomato salsa
makes/4 servings

½ pineapple, peeled, cored,
   and diced
1 mango, peeled, pitted, and diced
½ pint red pear tomatoes, halved
½ pint yellow pear
   tomatoes, halved
1 tablespoon chopped fresh
   cilantro
1 tablespoon olive oil

1. In a medium bowl combine pineapple, mango, tomato halves, and cilantro. Drizzle with olive oil.

sesame-crusted chilean sea bass

makes/4 servings • see photo, page 178

1 tablespoon olive oil
1 large egg
2 tablespoons heavy cream
1 cup white sesame seeds
2 pounds sea bass, cut into
   8-ounce portions
⅛ teaspoon salt
⅛ teaspoon black pepper
**Celery Root Purée (see recipe,
   opposite)**
**Super Simple Ponzu Sauce
   (see recipe, opposite)**

1. Preheat oven to 350°F. In a large skillet heat olive oil over medium heat.

2. In a bowl whisk egg and cream together. Place sesame seeds in a shallow dish.

3. Season sea bass with salt and pepper. Lightly brush egg mixture on the sea bass. Dip one side of the sea bass in sesame seeds.

4. Place sea bass, sesame seed sides down, in hot skillet. Let fish cook for 3 to 4 minutes or until sesame seeds are golden brown. Sprinkle olive oil on a baking sheet. Place sea bass on prepared baking sheet, sesame seed side up. Bake for 10 to 15 minutes or until fish is opaque.

5. To serve, place Celery Root Purée in the middle of a serving dish. Place sea bass on top of purée. Drizzle Super Simple Ponzu Sauce over sea bass and Celery Root Purée.

celery root purée
makes/4 to 6 servings • see photo, page 178

2 cups port wine
3 tablespoons packed brown
   sugar
1 teaspoon ground cinnamon
1 teaspoon ground nutmeg
2 pounds celery root
⅛ teaspoon salt
⅛ teaspoon black pepper

1. In a small saucepan stir together port wine, brown sugar, cinnamon, and nutmeg; bring to a boil over medium heat. Simmer for 30 minutes. Set aside to cool at room temperature.

2. Meanwhile, bring a large pot of water to a boil. Peel celery root and cut into cubes. Place cubes in boiling water; boil for 10 to 15 minutes or until tender. Drain.

3. In the pot or a bowl, mash celery root (using the same procedure as if you were making mashed potatoes). Season with salt and pepper; mix well. Stir port wine reduction into Celery Root Purée.

G's NOTES
This potato-like vegetable may also be used as a side dish.

super simple ponzu sauce
makes/4 servings • see photo, page 178

1 cup soy sauce
¾ cup orange juice
½ cup rice wine vinegar
⅓ cup honey
2 limes, juiced
2 tablespoons unsalted butter

1. Place all ingredients in a saucepan. Bring to a boil; reduce heat and let simmer for 15 minutes. Whisk in butter.

pistachio-crusted halibut
with lemon-chardonnay sauce
makes/4 servings

1½ cups finely chopped pistachios
4 8-ounce pieces skinless
   halibut fillet
   Kosher salt
   Black pepper
1 egg white, lightly beaten
⅓ cup olive oil
2 tablespoons unsalted butter
2 tablespoons chopped shallot
2 teaspoons chopped garlic
1 cup Chardonnay wine
1 tablespoon lemon juice
2 teaspoons chopped fresh parsley
   Herbed Israeli Couscous (see
   recipe, opposite)

1. Place pistachios in a shallow dish; set aside. Season halibut with salt and pepper. Brush egg white onto halibut.

2. In a sauté pan heat olive oil over medium heat. Press meat sides of halibut into pistachios, coating well. Add halibut to pan, coated sides down; sauté until golden. Remove from pan and keep warm.

3. Add butter, shallot, and garlic to pan; sauté for 1 minute. Add Chardonnay and lemon juice to pan; simmer until the liquid is reduced by half. Stir parsley into sauce.

4. To serve, place Herbed Israeli Couscous in center of plate. Top with halibut and spoon sauce over halibut and around the plate.

herbed israeli couscous

makes/4 servings

1 tablespoon olive oil
1 tablespoon chopped garlic
1 tablespoon chopped shallot
1 tablespoon chopped
   fresh parsley
1 tablespoon chopped fresh basil
1 teaspoon chopped fresh thyme
1 teaspoon chopped fresh oregano
1 cup uncooked Israeli couscous
2 cups chicken stock
½ cup diced tomato
   Zest of 1 lemon
1 tablespoon unsalted
   butter
1 fresh mint leaf

1. In a small saucepan heat olive oil over medium heat. Add garlic, shallot, parsley, basil, thyme, and oregano; sauté lightly. Stir in couscous. Add chicken stock.

2. Bring to a boil; reduce heat. Cover and simmer for 15 to 20 minutes or until liquid is absorbed and couscous is tender. Check frequently to make sure you have enough liquid.* Stir in tomato, lemon zest, and butter. Garnish with mint leaf.

* As with risotto, couscous absorbs a lot of liquid. Check it to make sure the liquid doesn't all get absorbed before the couscous is tender. If it cooks down too fast, add more hot chicken stock to the pot.

 G's NOTES

Israeli couscous, also referred to as pearls, is a larger version of the standard Mediterranean couscous. The cooking time is longer; however, the process is the same.

pan-seared scallops with **morel mushroom** sauce

makes/4 servings

1   pound medium scallops
1   teaspoon salt
1   teaspoon black pepper
2   tablespoons + 1 teaspoon
        olive oil
     Soy-Ginger Ponzu Sauce
        (see recipe, opposite)
6   whole morel mushrooms, halved,
        then each half cut into thirds
1   tablespoon unsalted butter
1   teaspoon chopped fresh
        Italian parsley
     Polenta (see recipe, opposite)
½   cup mixed greens
     Pinch salt

1. Rinse scallops and place on a cutting board. Sprinkle with salt and pepper. In a sauté pan heat 2 tablespoons of the olive oil over medium heat. Gently add scallops and sauté for 3 to 4 minutes per side or until golden brown, being careful not to overcook them.

2. Pour in ½ cup of the ponzu sauce. Add the morel mushrooms, butter, and parsley. Stir until butter is completely melted.

3. Place scallops on a serving plate in a circle, leaving the middle open to spoon in Polenta. Spoon in Polenta into the middle of scallops.

4. In a mixing bowl combine the mixed greens, the remaining 1 teaspoon olive oil, and a pinch of salt. Mix together so greens are lightly coated with olive oil. Place mixed greens on top of polenta and press down to secure. Next place the mushrooms on top of scallops and finish by drizzling the pan sauce over the scallops.

G's NOTES

Morel mushrooms are highly perishable. If you are unable to find them fresh, then use dried. They store better dried and last longer. To reconstitute dried mushrooms, just place them in a sealed container with a little warm water for several minutes; drain the water and pat dry.

polenta

makes/4 servings

2 cups water
  Pinch salt
  Pinch black pepper
2 cups yellow cornmeal
2 cups chicken stock
1 cup heavy cream
¼ cup shredded Parmesan cheese
1 tablespoon unsalted butter
1 tablespoons olive oil
  Cracked white pepper

1. Place the water in a pot with a pinch of salt and pepper. Bring to a boil over high heat. Slowly add cornmeal, a little at a time, while stirring with a whisk. When all the cornmeal has been added, reduce heat. Stir chicken stock into pot. Continue cooking and stirring until polenta has a smooth consistency. Remove from heat.

2. In a separate saucepan combine cream, Parmesan cheese, butter, olive oil, and white pepper to taste. Bring to a boil; reduce heat. Fold in polenta until well incorporated.

G's NOTES

Be sure to cook polenta for at least 25 minutes or until smooth and creamy. It should not be gritty at all. More water may be added during the cooking process to ensure the polenta will cook to desired consistency.

soy-ginger ponzu sauce

makes/about 3 cups

¼ cup olive oil
⅓ cup chopped carrot
⅓ cup chopped celery
⅓ cup chopped onion
1 Granny Smith apple, cored and quartered
1 tablespoon thinly sliced fresh ginger
4 cups chicken stock
2 cups soy sauce
1 cup orange juice
¼ cup packed brown sugar
¼ cup rice wine vinegar
¼ cup honey

1. In a pot heat olive oil over medium-high heat. Add carrot, celery, and onion. Stir in apple and ginger. Add chicken stock, soy sauce, orange juice, brown sugar, rice wine vinegar, and honey; mix well. Bring to a boil. Boil until sauce is reduced and thickened. Strain sauce and discard the vegetables and apple.

G's NOTES

Ponzu sauce is a citrus-based sauce used in Japanese cuisine. It is used in many dishes as a dipping sauce or as a light dressing.

Boil the sauce until its volume is reduced by evaporation, which thickens its consistency and intensifies its flavor.

maine lobster

makes/4 servings

6   quarts water
½   cup white wine
2   white onions, chopped
2   stalks celery, chopped
2   carrots, chopped
5   fresh bay leaves
2   teaspoons olive oil
1   teaspoon whole peppercorns
1   teaspoon salt
2   large Maine lobsters
     Saffron Risotto (see recipe,
        opposite)
     Sautéed Spinach (see recipe,
        opposite)
1   lemon, halved
1   teaspoons chopped fresh
        Italian parsley

1. In an 8-quart pot bring water to boil over medium-high heat. Add wine, onion, celery, carrot, bay leaves, olive oil, peppercorns, and salt. Place one lobster in the pot and boil for 6 to 8 minutes or until completely pink and the flesh is white. Using tongs, remove cooked lobster from pot. Repeat with second lobster. Cool lobsters in an ice bath.

2. Remove the claw meat by first grasping the hinged piece of the claw. Rock it back and forth while simultaneously pulling slowly and firmly so the cartilage comes out. Crack the claws with a claw cracker or lay the claws on a clean towel and use a mallet to crack them. (Do not smash them; just crack the shell.) Peel off the shell and remove the claw meat. Use claw meat in Saffron Risotto.

3. Cut off the lobster tails with kitchen shears. Cut the tails in half by cutting right down the middle on the top and bottom. Serve tails on a bed of Saffron Risotto. Top with Sautéed Spinach. Squeeze juice from lemon halves over lobster and garnish with parsley.

G's NOTES

After removing the lobster meat from the shell, either sauté or grill the meat for more doneness.

saffron risotto
makes/4 servings

5	to 6 cups chicken broth
1	cup chopped onion
5	tablespoons olive oil
1	cup Arborio rice
1	tablespoon chopped garlic
	Small pinch saffron threads
3	tablespoons shredded Parmesan cheese
1	tablespoon butter, melted
2	teaspoons salt
2	teaspoons black pepper
	Maine Lobster claw meat (see recipe, opposite)
	Sautéed Spinach (see recipe, below)

1. In a medium pot bring broth to a boil; reduce heat to a simmer. In a medium saucepan heat 1 tablespoon of the olive oil over medium heat. Add ½ cup of the onion; sauté until soft but not brown. Stir in the rice, garlic, and saffron.

2. Increase heat to medium-high. Stir in ½ cup of the hot broth; simmer, stirring constantly. As the broth is absorbed, continue to add broth, ⅓ cup at a time, while stirring constantly. Save ¼ cup of the broth to use in Step 3. Cook until rice is three-quarters of the way done (just starting to get tender). Remove from heat.

3. In a second pot heat the remaining 4 tablespoons olive oil over low heat. Add the remaining ½ cup onion and sauté until tender. Add the partially cooked risotto and ¼ cup of the broth; cook and stir constantly until desired consistency is reached. Stir in Parmesan cheese, melted butter, salt, and pepper. Stir in lobster claw meat.

4. To serve, spoon risotto on a dinner plate. Top with lobster tail half. Spoon Sautéed Spinach on top of lobster tail.

sautéed spinach
makes/4 servings

¼	cup olive oil
¼	cup chopped onion
2	teaspoons unsalted butter
1	teasoon chopped garlic
1	pound fresh spinach
	Salt
	Black pepper

1. In a sauté pan heat olive oil over medium-high heat. Add onion, butter, and garlic. Add spinach; toss with tongs until wilted. Add salt and pepper to taste; toss to combine. Using tongs, place spinach on paper towels to absorb excess moisture.

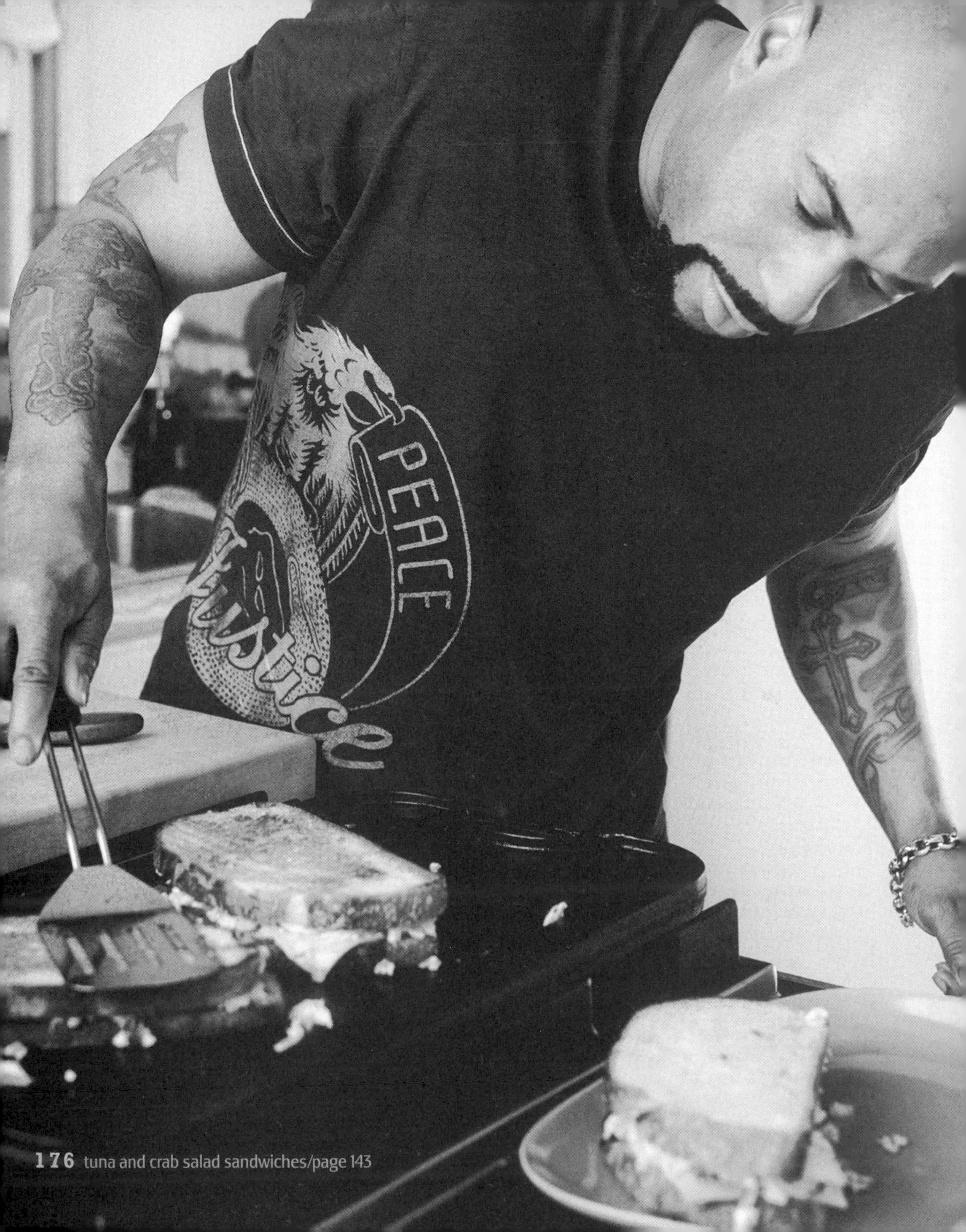

 tuna and crab salad sandwiches/page 143

178 sesame-crusted chilean sea bass with celery root
purée and super simple ponzu sauce/pages 168–169
haricots verts tied with chives/page 155

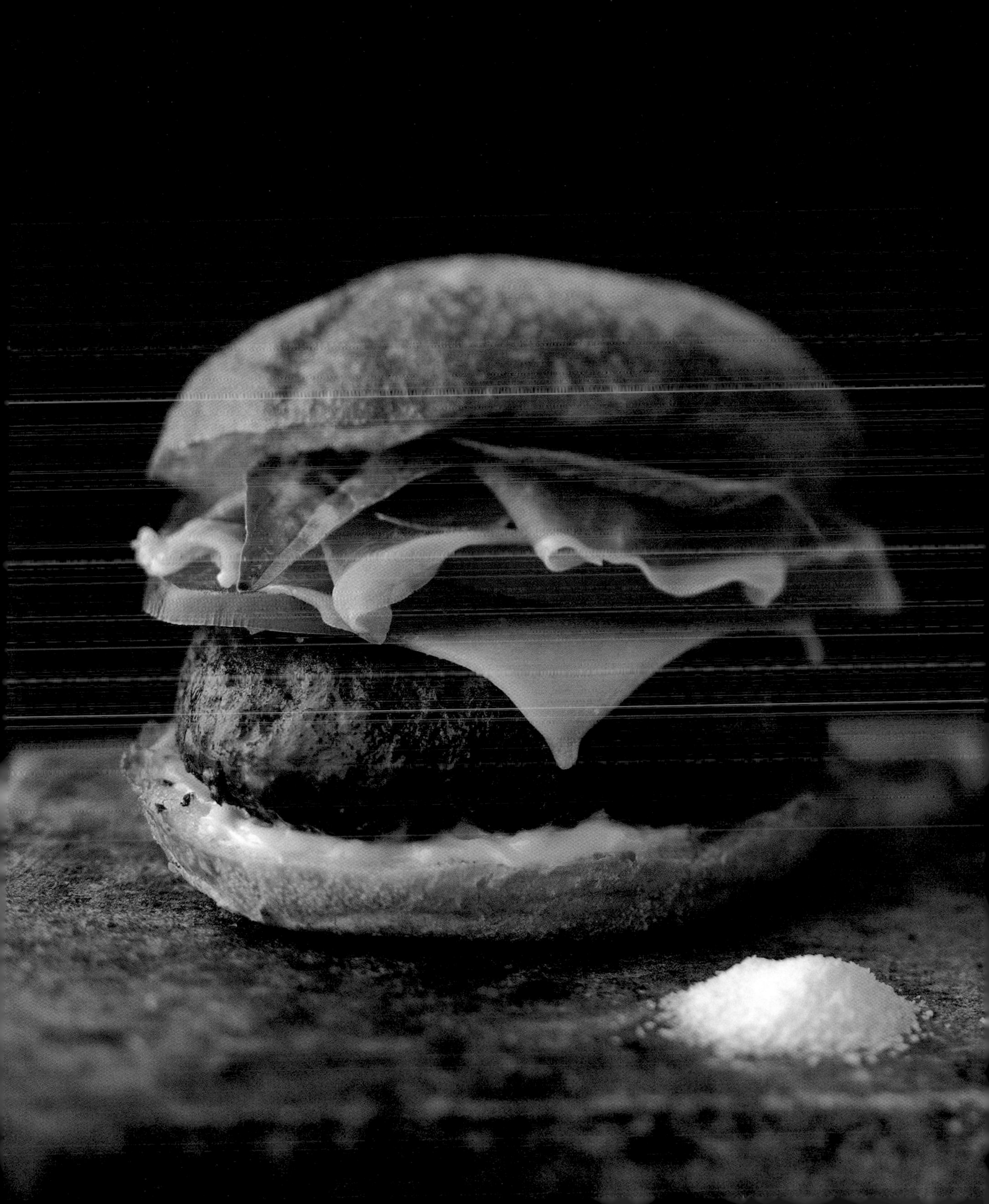

" Being in food is not just
a job for me. It's my life.
It's who I am, and that's
what you'll learn from this
book—exactly who I am. **"**

– Chef G. Garvin

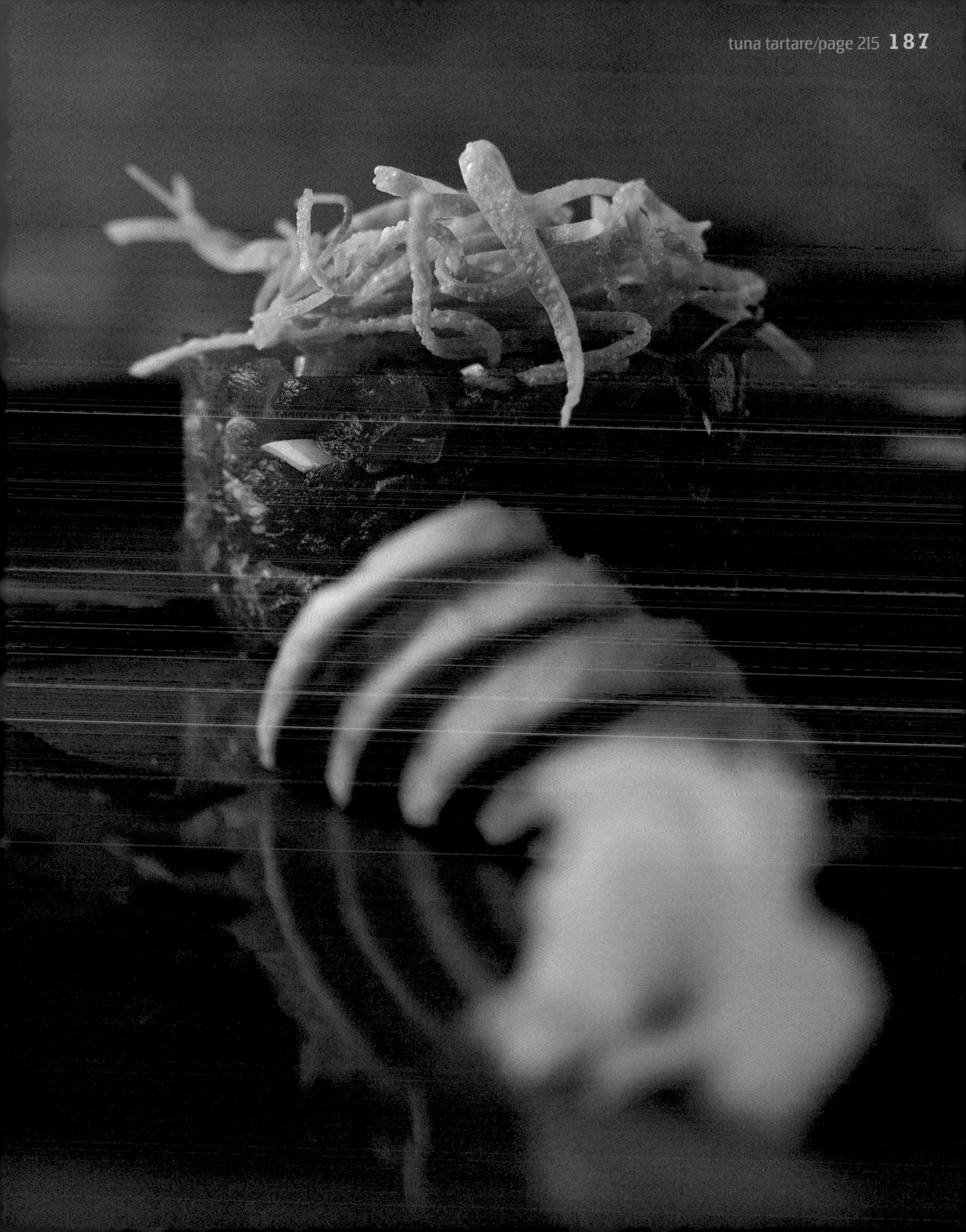

cognac, sticks, and steaks

{ Serve up tender, juicy burgers, steaks, and skewers that are down-right delicious. }

There are a lot of vegetarians nowadays that really enjoy themselves. I am not mad; do your thing. For me, though, it is a must that I have a great steak at least once a week. I am talking 16 ounces of dry-aged, perfectly grilled red meat, along with a couple sides, maybe some creamed corn or sautéed mushrooms—the works. I have a couple buddies in L.A.—Steve and Bryan, and on occasion a few more cats—who will head out and hit Mastro's, Dantanna's. Or I might just throw a few steaks on the grill at the house. Of course, after dinner, it is time for a good stick (cigar) and some adult conversation. My man D.L. Hughley and Red are always good for heated debates that at times reach a high level over a good stick. Guys' night out—there is nothing like it. But you best believe, it is real when it goes down.

blackened shrimp skewers

makes/10 to 15 skewers

8   ounces medium shrimp
10   to 15 wooden skewers,
     6 inches long
10   to 15 foil squares (4-inch squares)
1   tablespoon Blackening Spice
     (see recipe, page 139)
3   tablespoons olive oil

1. Clean shrimp, removing shells and veins. Take a skewer and push it lengthwise through a shrimp, starting at the tail. Repeat with remaining shrimp and skewers. Wrap ends of skewers with foil so they won't burn or get oily while preparing. Season skewered shrimp with Blackening Spice.

2. In a grill pan heat olive oil over medium heat. Grill skewers for 1 to 2 minutes per side or until shrimp are cooked through. Place skewers on serving plate; remove foil before serving.

homemade bourbon barbecue sauce

makes/5½ cups

2   tablespoons olive oil
3   tablespoons chopped
     jalapeño pepper
     (see tip, page 207)
2   tablespoons chopped garlic
2   tablespoons chopped shallot
2   cups ketchup
¼   cup bourbon
1   cup orange juice
1   cup molasses
¼   cup Coca-Cola®
1   cup packed brown sugar
1   teaspoon liquid smoke
1   teaspoon paprika
1   teaspoon garlic salt
1   teaspoon barbecue spice blend

1. In a sauté pan heat olive oil over medium heat. Add jalapeño, garlic, and shallot; sauté until browned.

2. Pour in ketchup, then the bourbon. (CAUTION: Using bourbon or any alcohol may ignite flames in the pan.) Stir in orange juice, molasses, and cola; mix well. Stir in remaining ingredients. Cook and stir until sugar is dissolved and sauce thickens.

bourbon barbecue **wings**

makes/8 to 12 servings

24 **chicken wings**
2 **teaspoons garlic salt**
2 **teaspoons salt**
2 **teaspoons black pepper**
3 **cups canola oil**
    Homemade Bourbon Barbecue Sauce (see recipe, opposite)

1. Rinse chicken wings. Split wings at joints into two parts. Cut off the tips. Season wings all over with garlic salt, salt, and pepper.

2. In a deep pan or deep fryer heat canola oil over medium-high heat. Fry chicken wings until golden brown and cooked thoroughly. Place wings on paper towels to soak up excess oil.

3. Place fried wings in Homemade Bourbon Barbecue Sauce; mix well. To serve, remove wings from sauce and place on a plate. Pour sauce liberally over top.

G's NOTES

For more flavor kick, place the fried wings in an oven-proof dish. Pour the barbecue sauce over the wings and bake in a 325°F. oven for 5 minutes.

g. garvin's **baby back ribs**

makes/6 to 8 servings • see photo, page 180

3 racks baby back ribs
1 cup barbecue
    spice blend
2 cups water
½ cup lemon juice
2 tablespoons honey
1 teaspoon liquid smoke
    Homemade Bourbon Barbecue
    Sauce (see recipe, page 196)

1. Sprinkle baby back ribs with ½ cup of the barbecue spice blend. Cover and refrigerate overnight.

2. Preheat oven to 250°F. In a bowl mix together the water, lemon juice, honey, liquid smoke, and remaining ½ cup barbecue spice blend.

3. Grill baby back ribs over medium-high direct heat for 2 to 5 minutes per side or until browned, basting them occasionally with lemon juice mixture.

4. Lay out four 2-foot-long sheets of foil, overlapping by 2 inches to form one large sheet. Place ribs together on sheet and wrap securely. Place on a large baking pan. Bake for 2½ hours or until meat is tender. Serve with Homemade Bourbon Barbecue Sauce.

 G's NOTES

This is the way I do my ribs. I'm just sharing my secret with you.

kicked-up burgers

makes/3 burgers • see photo, page 181

1   pound ground beef
3   tablespoons Worcestershire
    sauce
2   teaspoons chopped garlic
2   teaspoons chopped shallot
2   teaspoons chopped fresh
    Italian parsley
¼   teaspoon salt
    Pinch cayenne pepper
1   egg
1   teaspoon + 1 pinch black pepper
2   tablespoons bread crumbs
5   tablespoons olive oil
3   sourdough hamburger buns
3   tablespoons mayonnaise
3   teaspoons Dijon mustard
    Burger toppings (right)

1. In a large glass bowl combine ground beef, Worcestershire sauce, garlic, shallot, parsley, salt, and cayenne pepper. Add egg and 1 teaspoon black pepper; mix well. Add bread crumbs and mix again. Take one-third of meat mixture, roll it into a ball, then pat it down into a patty. Repeat to make two more patties.

2. In a sauté pan heat olive oil over medium-high heat. Add patties to pan. When one side is cooked halfway through, flip the burgers so the other side can cook.

3. Open 3 sourdough buns and spread 1 tablespoon mayonnaise and 1 teaspoon mustard on each bun. Sprinkle with a pinch of black pepper. Place a burger on the bottom of each bun. Add desired burger toppings and the tops of the buns.

avocado burger toppings:
3 slices tomato
1 avocado, peeled, pitted, and sliced
6 slices onion
6 slices Gruyère cheese

crispy bacon and blue cheese burger toppings:
3 slices tomato
9 slices bacon, fried crisp
6 slices blue cheese

prosciutto burger toppings:
3 slices tomato
3 slices prosciutto
3 slices blue cheese
3 fresh basil leaves

asian-style filet

makes/4 servings

¾ cup soy sauce
¼ cup rice wine vinegar
¼ cup chili oil
¼ cup sesame oil
4 6-ounce pieces filet mignon
¼ cup olive oil
4 whole scallions
4 cloves garlic
¾ cup orange juice
¼ cup lemon juice
¼ cup lime juice
¼ cup honey
1 tablespoon packed brown sugar
3 tablespoons cornstarch
3 tablespoons water
2 pinches sesame seeds
4 slices pickled ginger
Pinch black pepper

1. In a large bowl combine ¼ cup of the soy sauce, the rice wine vinegar, chili oil, and sesame oil; mix well. Place filets in marinade; let stand for about 5 minutes.

2. In a grill pan heat olive oil over medium-high heat. Remove filets from marinade and place in grill pan with scallions and garlic. Grill until filets, scallions, and garlic are desired doneness. Remove from grill pan and set aside.

3. For sauce, in a saucepan combine orange juice, the remaining ½ cup soy sauce, the lemon juice, lime juice, honey, and brown sugar. Bring to a simmer over medium-high heat. In a small bowl combine cornstarch and water. Stir cornstarch mixture into saucepan. Reduce heat and stir until sauce is thickened.

4. To serve, plate filets with scallions and garlic. Spoon sauce over top. Garnish with sesame seeds, pickled ginger, and pepper.

 G's NOTES

If you like, you can reserve the marinade and combine with the sauce ingredients and cook as directed in step 3.

grilled **filet mignon** with shiitake mushroom red wine sauce

makes/4 servings

4   **8-ounce pieces filet mignon**
1   **teaspoon salt**
1   **teaspoon black pepper**
¼   **cup olive oil**
2   **tablespoons chopped garlic**
2   **tablespoons chopped shallot**
6   **fresh shiitake mushrooms, sliced**
1   **teaspoon unsalted butter**
1   **cup red wine**
2   **tablespoons heavy cream**
2   **tablespoons honey**
     Hot cooked rice

1. Season filets with the salt and pepper. Pat seasonings into meat. Set aside.

2. In a sauté pan heat olive oil over medium-high heat. Add filets and sear on both sides. Add garlic, shallot, and mushrooms to pan. Stir in butter until melted. Add wine, cream, and honey; bring to a simmer.

3. To serve, place filets on rice. Spoon pan sauce over top.

filet mignon and **fingerling potatoes**

makes/2 large or 4 small servings

2	cups fingerling potatoes
4	tablespoons olive oil
3	teaspoons chopped garlic
3	teaspoons chopped shallot
3½	teaspoons kosher salt
3½	teaspoons black pepper
2	cups broccoli florets
2	8-ounce pieces filet mignon
4	scallions
6	ounces crumbled blue cheese

1. In a large pot bring 3 quarts water to a boil. Add potatoes and boil for 10 minutes. Using a slotted spoon, remove potatoes from the pot and let cool. Cut potatoes in half and place in a bowl. Add 1 tablespoon of the olive oil and 1½ teaspoons each of the garlic, shallot, salt, and pepper; toss to coat. Set aside.

2. To boiling water add the broccoli. Boil for 1 minute. Remove broccoli from pot and place in a bowl of ice water. Drain. Place broccoli in a bowl with 1 tablespoon of the olive oil and 1½ teaspoons each of the garlic, shallot, salt, and pepper; toss to coat. Set aside.

3. Season filet mignon with the remaining ½ teaspoon each salt and pepper. In a grill pan heat the remaining 2 tablespoons olive oil over medium heat. Add filets and cook for 5 to 6 minutes per side or until desired doneness.

4. Add potatoes, broccoli, and scallions to the grill pan. Grill until potatoes are browned. Top steaks with blue cheese. Place filets on a plate along with potatoes, broccoli, and scallions.

steak au poivre

makes/4 servings

¼   cup olive oil
4   10-ounce New York strip steaks
    Salt
½   cup cracked black pepper
2   tablespoons chopped garlic
2   tablespoons chopped shallot
3   tablespoons unsalted butter
¼   cup brandy
½   cup red wine
2   tablespoons Chambord black
      raspberry liqueur
⅓   cup heavy cream
    Asparagus and Potatoes
      (see recipe, below)

1. Preheat oven to 350°F. In a large sauté pan heat olive oil over medium-high heat. Season steaks to taste with salt. Coat steaks with cracked pepper, pressing pepper into the meat to make sure it sticks. Sear steaks in pan for 3 to 4 minutes per side.

2. Transfer steaks to a baking pan and place in oven. Cook for 10 to 15 minutes or until desired doneness.

3. In the same sauté pan sauté garlic and shallot in 2 tablespoons of the butter until light brown. Remove pan from heat and add brandy. Return to heat. Add red wine; simmer for 3 minutes. Drizzle in Chambord. Stir in cream. Finish by stirring in the remaining 1 tablespoon butter until melted. Pour sauce over steaks. Serve with Asparagus and Potatoes.

asparagus and potatoes

makes/4 servings

4   tablespoons olive oil
2   teaspoons chopped garlic
2   teaspoons chopped shallot
1   pound fingerling potatoes,
      blanched and halved
    Salt
    Black pepper
8   ounce bunch fresh asparagus

1. In a sauté pan heat 2 tablespoons of the olive oil over medium heat. Add 1 teaspoon of the garlic and 1 teaspoon of the shallot; sauté for 1 to 2 minutes. Add potato halves to the pan; sauté until golden brown. Season to taste with salt and black pepper. Remove from pan and keep warm. Repeat procedure for asparagus.

porterhouse with **hearty vegetables**
makes/4 servings

2   12-ounce porterhouse steaks
2   teaspoons + 2 tablespoons salt
1   teaspoon freshly ground
      black pepper
7   tablespoons olive oil
½   cup diced red potato
¼   cup chopped celery
¼   cup sliced carrot
¼   cup chopped onion
¼   cup white wine
4   whole shallots
10 cloves garlic
2   tablespoons whole black
      peppercorns
5   stems rosemary leaves

1. Heat oven to 350°F. Season steaks on both sides with 2 teaspoons of the salt and the freshly ground pepper.

2. In a heavy roasting pot heat 4 tablespoons of the olive oil over medium-high heat. Add steaks and sear lightly on both sides. Add potato, celery, carrot, onion, white wine, shallots, garlic, peppercorns, rosemary, the remaining 3 tablespoons olive oil, and the remaining 2 tablespoons salt to pan.

3. Place pan in oven and roast, uncovered, for 20 minutes. Remove from oven and serve in pan.

cracked black pepper steak and blue cheese
makes/4 servings

2 10-ounce New York strip steaks
2 teaspoons salt
3 tablespoons cracked
    black pepper
¼ cup olive oil
    Blue cheese, crumbled
    Chopped fresh parsley
    Black pepper

1. Heat oven to 350°F. Season steaks on both sides with salt and cracked pepper, pressing pepper into the meat to make sure it sticks.

2. In an oven-safe sauté pan heat olive oil over medium-high heat. Add steaks to pan and brown on both sides. Place pan in oven for 10 minutes. Remove steaks from oven and top with blue cheese. Return the steaks to oven for 3 minutes.

3. To serve, cut steaks into thin slices. Plate steaks, then garnish with parsley and black pepper.

bbq **salmon**
makes/4 servings

4   8-ounce pieces salmon fillet, skin removed
1½ teaspoons lemon-pepper seasoning
    Pinch salt
2   tablespoons olive oil
1   tablespoon chopped garlic
1   tablespoon chopped shallot
1   cup Homemade Bourbon Barbecue Sauce (see recipe, page 196)

1. Preheat oven to 350°F. Season both sides of salmon with lemon-pepper seasoning and salt. In an ovenproof sauté pan heat olive oil over medium heat. Add garlic and shallot; sauté for 1 minute. Place salmon in skillet and cook for 3 minutes per side.

2. Pour barbecue sauce over salmon. Place pan in oven for 5 minutes or until salmon is desired doneness.

king crab legs
makes/6 to 8 servings

2   quarts water
2   tablespoons lemon juice
1   tablespoon kosher salt
1   tablespoon black pepper
2   to 3 pounds king crab legs
¼   cup olive oil
2   tablespoons chopped garlic
    Pinch cayenne pepper
½   cup (1 stick) salted butter, melted

1. In a large pot combine water, lemon juice, salt, and black pepper. Bring to a boil.

2. With a pair of kitchen shears or lobster scissors, cut slits along the lighter-color side of the crab leg shells to make them easy to split later. Add the crab legs to the boiling water; boil for 5 to 7 minutes or until crab is cooked through.

3. In a large bowl combine olive oil, garlic, cayenne pepper, and salt and black pepper to taste. Add crab legs and toss well to coat.

4. Remove crab legs from bowl, draining excess oil. Grill crab legs over medium direct heat for 5 to 7 minutes or until heated through. Serve crab legs with melted butter for dipping.

jerked lobster tail and jerked snapper
makes/4 servings

Jerk Seasoning (see recipe, below)

2 6- to 8-ounce lobster tails
2 6- to 8-ounce snapper fillets
   Olive oil
   Hot cooked rice

1. Spread jerk seasoning over lobster tails and snapper fillets; marinate for 3 hours.

2. Preheat grill or grill pan. Rub olive oil over jerked seafood. Grill lobster tail for 2 to 3 minutes per side. Grill snapper fillets for 3 to 4 minutes per side. Serve over rice.

jerk seasoning
makes/1¾ cups

1   large onion, chopped
½   cup packed brown sugar
4   scallions, chopped
1   to 3 Scotch bonnet peppers, seeded and chopped*
2   tablespoons olive oil
2   tablespoons soy sauce
2   tablespoons lime juice
2   teaspoons salt
1   teaspoon ground cinnamon
½   teaspoon ground allspice
½   teaspoon dried thyme
½   teaspoon ground nutmeg
⅛   teaspoon ground cloves

1. Combine all ingredients in a food processor and process until uniform, or finely chop all ingredients and mix well.

* When handling hot chile peppers, such as jalapeños and Scotch bonnet peppers, it is strongly recommended that you wear gloves. Do not touch your face, rub your eyes, or touch any other part of your body until you wash your hands thoroughly, scrubbing under your nails, etc.

G's NOTES
Although this recipe is set up for a food processor, the onion, scallions, and the seeded Scotch bonnet pepper may be chopped by hand and mixed well with the other ingredients.

entertaining
with *G*

{ G's party-perfect foods look impressive,
taste delicious, and don't take long to make. }

Entertaining at home is always a big deal for me. I just love doing it—going to the flower market for beautiful fresh flowers that I put together myself and place all over the house, bringing out the good glassware and silver, busting out the cookware. On this night, pull out the slacks or a sexy skirt; add a great dress shirt or top. (For guys, try cuff links but no tie.) Most of all, remember that entertaining is all about setting up a great-looking table that just fills the universe with this amazing positive energy. And don't forget about after-dinner activities. Set the room for a great stick (cigar) and cognac for the gentlemen, maybe some cappuccino and cookies for the ladies. Play some Marvin Gaye, a little Frank, and some Miles Davis. It's a beautiful thing ...

shrimp and beef skewers
makes/8 servings • see photo, page 185

1   **pound medium shrimp**
2   **teaspoons salt**
2   **teaspoons black pepper**
1⅛ **teaspoons Blackening Spice**
      (see recipe, page 139)
6   **tablespoons olive oil**
      Wooden skewers, 6 inches long
1   **pound filet mignon**

1. Clean shrimp, removing shells and veins. Season shrimp with 1 teaspoon of the salt, 1 teaspoon of the pepper, and 1 teaspoon of the Blackening Spice. Sprinkle 1 tablespoon of the olive oil over shrimp. Take a skewer and push it lengthwise through a shrimp, starting at the tail. Repeat with remaining shrimp; set aside.

2. Slice beef into 3×1-inch strips. Season beef with the remaining salt, pepper, and Blackening Spice. Thread meat strips accordian-style onto skewers; set aside.

3. In a grill pan heat the remaining 5 tablespoons olive oil over medium-high heat. Add shrimp and beef skewers to grill pan, allowing skewer ends to hang off the sides of the pan. Cook shrimp skewers about 5 minutes and the beef to your liking, turning skewers over once so they cook evenly. Remove skewers from pan and place on paper towels to absorb excess oil.

smoked salmon with kettle chips,
sour cream, and horseradish sauce

makes/4 to 6 servings • see photo, page 186

3 tablespoons sour cream
2 teaspoons horseradish
1 teaspoon chopped garlic
1 teaspoon chopped shallot
1 teaspoon black pepper
⅛ teaspoon salt
½ lemon, juiced
1 large bag potato chips
1 8-ounce package sliced, smoked,
    and cured salmon
  Chopped fresh chives

1. In a medium bowl combine sour cream, horseradish, garlic, shallot, pepper, and salt; mix well. Squeeze lemon juice* into bowl; stir in.

2. Place several flat potato chips on a serving dish. Add a small dollop of sour cream mixture to center of each chip.

3. Cut salmon slices into strips. Roll up strips and place on top of sour cream dollops on chips. Sprinkle fresh chives on each for garnish.

* To get the most juice out of a lemon, use the palm of your hand to roll a whole lemon on a hard surface before halving.

G's NOTES
I recommend using kettle potato chips in this recipe.

fresh crab **cigars**
makes/24 cigars

24 wonton wrappers
1 large egg
3 tablespoons heavy cream
½ cup lump crabmeat
3 tablespoons hot sauce
3 tablespoons Worcestershire
   sauce
2 tablespoons mayonnaise
2 tablespoons Dijon mustard
1 tablespoon diced red bell
   pepper, sautéed
1 tablespoon diced orange bell
   peppers, sautéed
1 tablespoon diced green bell
   peppers, sautéed
2 teaspoons Old Bay® seasoning
½ cup cornstarch
   Vegetable oil

1. Place wonton wrappers on a damp paper towel and cover with a second damp paper towel; set aside until ready to use. Crack egg into a small bowl. Add heavy cream and beat together until smooth. Set egg wash aside.

2. In a medium glass bowl combine crabmeat, hot sauce, Worcestershire sauce, mayonnaise, Dijon mustard, bell pepper, and Old Bay seasoning; mix well. Set crab filling aside.

3. Place a wonton wrapper on work surface with corner pointing at you (diamond shape). With a brush, brush egg wash onto edges of wrapper. Place 1 teaspoon crab filling in center of wrapper. Roll wrapper around the filling, folding the sides inward to resemble a cigar. Repeat with remaining wonton wrappers and crab filling.

4. Place cornstarch on a plate; roll cigars in cornstarch. (The cornstarch allows the egg wash to dry.)

5. Heat 3 inches of vegetable oil in a deep fryer to 350°F. Drop cigars into oil and fry until golden brown. Place cigars on paper towels to absorb excess oil.

G's NOTES
The moisture from the damp paper towel will allow the wonton wrappers to stay moist and not dry out.

seared scallops with tomato
ragoût and caramelized onions

makes/4 servings • see photo, page 179

3 tablespoons olive oil
8 ounces sea scallops
   Salt
   Black pepper
1 tablespoon chopped shallot
1 tablespoon chopped garlic
4 pieces canned plum tomatoes
¼ cup white wine
1 tablespoon honey
¼ teaspoon chopped fresh thyme
   Caramelized Shallots (see
     recipe, right)
1 head frisée
   Chive Oil (see recipe, right)
   Chive sprigs

1. In a sauté pan heat 2 tablespoons of the olive oil over medium-high heat. Season scallops to taste with salt and pepper. Sear scallops on both sides in hot pan; remove from pan. Set aside and keep warm.

2. For ragoût, in the same pan sauté shallot in the remaining 1 tablespoon olive oil until golden brown. Add garlic and sauté until slightly brown. Add tomatoes, white wine, honey, and thyme; mix well. Cook for 5 minutes, stirring occasionally.

3. Return scallops to pan and heat through. Arrange scallops around the outside of the serving plate. Spoon Caramelized Shallots on top of each scallop. Spoon ragoût around the scallops. Garnish with frisée and a drizzle of the Chive Oil around the outside of the scallops. Garnish with chive sprigs.

caramelized shallots: In a sauté pan heat 2 tablespoons unsalted butter and 1 tablespoon olive oil over medium heat. Add 6 to 8 sliced shallots; sauté until brown. Add 1 tablespoon packed brown sugar and stir until melted. Add 2 tablespoons red wine, 2 tablespoons balsamic vinegar, 1 teaspoon chopped fresh thyme, and salt and black pepper to taste. Simmer for 3 to 5 minutes or until liquid is nearly absorbed. Set aside.

chive oil: Remove a few sprigs of chives from a bunch of chives for garnish. Chop the remainder of the bunch and place in a food processor. Pulse chives until very finely chopped (nearly liquid). Pour in ½ cup olive oil and let sit for 20 minutes. Strain oil through cheesecloth. Set aside until ready to use. Drizzle oil with a spoon or dispense from a small squeeze bottle.

tuna **tartare**
makes/4 servings • see photo, page 187

4   3-ounce pieces tuna loin
⅓   cup + 2 teaspoons seasoned rice vinegar
¼   cup soy sauce
2   tablespoons sesame oil
4   teaspoons sliced scallion
2   teaspoons chopped shallot
    Pinch salt
    Pinch black pepper
1   avocado, pitted, peeled, and sliced
12   whole chives
4   to 8 pieces pickled ginger
2   teaspoons chili oil
4   wonton wrappers (optional)
    Sesame oil (optional)

1. Chop tuna very finely and place in a medium bowl. Add ⅓ cup of the vinegar, the soy sauce, sesame oil, scallion, shallot, salt, and pepper; mix well.

2. Place a 2-inch metal ring mold in the center of a serving dish. Fill ring with one-fourth of tuna mixture and pat with spoon to make it firm. Carefully remove ring from around tuna mixture. Repeat to make 3 more servings.

3. Arrange avocado around the sides of tuna molds. Top tuna with chives and pickled ginger. Drizzle with chili oil and the remaining 2 teaspoons vinegar.

4. If desired, serve Tuna Tartare with toasted wonton wrappers. To toast wonton wrappers, brush them with additional sesame oil and bake in a 325°F oven until slightly browned.

 's NOTES
When buying tuna, don't buy tuna that has been stored directly on ice. This will bleed out the color.

lobster bisque
makes/8 to 10 servings

½ cup olive oil
2 pounds lobster bodies
   and heads, split and cut up*
6 cloves garlic, smashed
6 shallots, rough chopped
2 tablespoons tomato paste
½ head celery, cut up into 8 pieces
3 carrots, cut up into 8 pieces
2 onions, cut up into large dice
1 cup brandy
8 cups chicken stock
2 cups heavy cream
1 tablespoon salt
1½ teaspoons black pepper
3 bay leaves
3 sprigs fresh thyme
½ cup (1 stick) unsalted butter

1. In a large stockpot heat olive oil over medium-high heat. When oil is slightly smoky, add lobster parts and sauté for several minutes until pink.

2. Add garlic and shallot. Add tomato paste and mix thoroughly, making sure the paste is sautéed. Add celery, carrot, and onion. Cook until vegetables start to get soft around the edges.

3. Remove pot from heat and add brandy. (Brandy is extremely flammable, so be careful.) Return pot to heat and cook for 3 minutes more. Add chicken stock and cream. Bring to a boil, then reduce heat to a simmer. Add salt, pepper, bay leaves, and thyme. Simmer for 30 minutes.

4. Remove from heat and strain; discard solids. Return bisque to heat and simmer for 10 minutes more. To finish, whisk in butter until melted.

* Get lobster from your local seafood market. Have the market split them.

cauliflower, white rose potato, and crab bisque with **truffle oil**

makes/4 servings

3	tablespoons olive oil
½	cup diced onion
2	tablespoons chopped garlic
1	tablespoon chopped shallot
1	head cauliflower, chopped small
2	white rose potatoes, peeled and diced
	Salt
	White pepper
½	cup white wine
4	cups chicken stock
2	cups water
2	cups heavy cream
2	tablespoons unsalted butter
8	ounces cooked crabmeat
	White truffle oil
	Sliced scallion

1. In a medium pot heat olive oil over medium heat. Add onion, garlic, and shallot; sauté until soft but not colored. Add cauliflower and potato. Season with salt and pepper.

2. Add white wine and cook for 2 to 3 minutes. Add chicken stock and water; bring to a simmer. Simmer for 10 to 15 minutes or until cauliflower and potato are tender. Add cream; simmer for 5 minutes more.

3. In a food processor place half of the cauliflower mixture and 1 tablespoon of the butter; pulse until smooth. Place in a second pot and repeat with remaining cauliflower mixture and butter. Taste and adjust seasonings, if necessary.

4. Add crabmeat to bisque and heat for 5 minutes. When bisque is hot, ladle into bowls and garnish with a drizzle of truffle oil and some sliced scallion.

G's NOTES
If you are not a fan of crabmeat, prepare the recipe without it.

arugula salad with parmesan cheese crisps
makes/4 to 6 servings

16 ounces baby arugula
1   teaspoon salt
1   teaspoon black pepper
1   teaspoon chopped garlic
1   teaspoon chopped shallot
1   16-ounce block Parmesan cheese
    Citrus Vinaigrette 2
      (see recipe, below)
    Balsamic vinegar (optional)

1. Preheat oven to 375°F. Rinse arugula under water. Place in a bowl. Season arugula with salt, pepper, garlic, and shallot. Toss to combine; set aside.

2. Grate block of cheese. Pat cheese into small rounded shapes on a nonstick baking sheet or a baking sheet lined with parchment paper. Bake for 3 to 4 minutes or until cheese is melted and golden. Remove from oven and set aside.

3. Pour Citrus Vinaigrette 2 over arugula and toss to coat. Break cheese crisps in half and place on arugula. If desired, drizzle a tablespoon of balsamic vinegar over salad.

citrus vinaigrette 2
makes/about 1½ cups

¼   cup rice wine vinegar
2   lemons, juiced
¼   cup orange juice
1   tablespoon chopped shallot
1½ teaspoons chopped garlic
1   teaspoon salt
1   teaspoon black pepper
¾   cup olive oil

1. In a bowl combine rice wine vinegar, lemon juice, orange juice, shallot, garlic, salt, and pepper. Whisk in olive oil.

fried **goat cheese** salad with a white truffle oil drizzle

makes/4 servings

1   cup all-purpose flour
1   cup dried bread crumbs
1   teaspoon chopped fresh
      rosemary
1   teaspoon chopped fresh thyme
    Salt
    Black pepper
½   cup heavy cream
1   egg
½   cup olive oil
1   7-ounce log goat cheese (chèvre)
1   head endive
    Mesclun greens
6   sugar plums, cut in
      half and cored
    Caramelized Walnuts (see recipe,
      below)
½   cup Balsamic Vinaigrette
      (see recipe, page 20)
    White truffle oil

1. Place flour on a flat plate. Place bread crumbs on a second plate, mixing in rosemary, thyme, and salt and pepper to taste. In a shallow dish make an egg wash by lightly beating together the cream and egg.

2. In a skillet heat olive oil over medium heat. Season the log of goat cheese with salt and pepper. Slice the cheese into ½ inch rounds. Dredge cheese slices in the flour, dip into egg wash, then dredge in the bread crumbs. Place pieces in hot oil and fry for 15 to 20 seconds on each side or until golden brown. Place fried goat cheese on a plate lined with paper towels to absorb excess oil.

3. To assemble the salad, arrange endive leaves on a large plate. Add mesclun greens to middle of plate. Arrange sugar plums on salad. Sprinkle Caramelized Walnuts over salad. Finally place goat cheese on the plate. Drizzle Balsamic Vinaigrette over the salad, then drizzle lightly with white truffle oil to finish.

caramelized **walnuts**

makes/1 cup • serve with fried goat cheese salad with a white truffle oil drizzle

¼   cup unsalted butter
¼   cup packed brown sugar
1   cup walnuts

1. Preheat oven to 350°F. Heat a sauté pan over medium heat. Add butter to pan and let the butter melt. Add brown sugar and mix well. Add walnuts and stir until evenly coated with sugar mixture.

2. Place walnuts on a nonstick baking sheet or a baking sheet covered with parchment paper. Bake for 5 to 10 minutes or until sugar bubbles and caramelizes on nuts. Remove from oven and allow to cool. Once cool, crumble walnuts and set aside.

G's NOTES
The sugar gets very hot. Don't touch it while it's hot.

holiday **cornish hen**

makes/4 large or 8 small servings

1   **tablespoon kosher salt**
1   **tablespoon black pepper**
1   **tablespoon seasoned salt**
1   **tablespoon garlic salt**
1   **tablespoon cayenne pepper**
1   **tablespoon dried rosemary**
1   **tablespoon chopped garlic**
1   **tablespoon dried thyme**
4   **Cornish game hens**
2   **tablespoons olive oil**
    Salt
    Black pepper
    Wild Rice (see recipe, opposite)

1. Preheat oven to 350°F. In a small bowl combine salt, black pepper, seasoned salt, garlic salt, cayenne pepper, rosemary, garlic, and thyme. Set spice blend aside.

2. Rinse Cornish hens under cold water. Season hens with spice blend, rubbing spices all over hens. Set aside.

3. In a roasting pan heat olive oil over medium heat. Place hens in pan and sprinkle with additional salt and black pepper. Sear hens on all sides until golden brown. Transfer pan to oven for 20 to 30 minutes or until temperature in thigh muscle registers 160°F. Serve with Wild Rice.

wild rice
makes/8 to 10 servings

2 tablespoons olive oil
½ cup chopped celery
2 tablespoons chopped garlic
2 tablespoons chopped shallot
¼ cup unsalted butter
2 cups uncooked wild rice
¼ cup wild rice seasoning* (usually found in box with wild rice)
 Pinch black pepper
2 cups chicken stock
8 ounces raisins
8 ounces dried cranberries
2 tablespoons chopped fresh parsley
1 tablespoon garlic salt

1. In a saucepan heat olive oil over medium heat. Add celery, garlic, shallot, and butter; mix well. Stir in wild rice, wild rice seasoning, and pepper. Add chicken stock. Bring to a boil; cover. Reduce heat and let simmer until all the liquid is absorbed.

2. When all of the liquid is gone, add raisins, cranberries, parsley, and garlic salt; mix together.

* If desired, omit the wild rice seasoning, black pepper, and chicken stock and substitute 2 cups water, 1 tablespoon chicken base, 1 teaspoon seasoned salt, 1 teaspoon onion powder, and 1 teaspoon poultry seasoning.

pan-roasted veal chops with morel sauce

makes/4 servings • see photo, page 184

¼ cup + 2 teaspoons olive oil
4 veal chops, ½ inch thick
3 tablespoons unsalted butter
2 tablespoons chopped garlic
2 tablespoons chopped shallot
1 teaspoon chopped fresh
 rosemary
10 whole morel mushrooms,
 diced large
½ cup red wine
½ cup white wine
½ cup chicken stock
½ cup heavy cream
 Salt
 Black pepper
 Parmesan Risotto (see recipe,
 opposite)
 Seared Foie Gras (see recipe,
 opposite)

1. Preheat oven to 350°F. In a large sauté pan heat ¼ cup of the olive oil over medium-high heat. Sear veal chops on both sides in hot pan. Place chops on an ungreased baking sheet and roast in the oven for 10 minutes.

2. Meanwhile, in the same sauté pan heat 2 tablespoons of the butter and the remaining 2 teaspoons olive oil over medium heat. Add garlic, shallot, and rosemary; sauté just until golden. Stir in morel mushrooms. Deglaze pan with red wine and white wine, stirring to loosen browned bits on bottom of pan. Stir in chicken stock and cream. Simmer until sauce is reduced and thickened. Finish sauce by stirring in the remaining 1 tablespoon butter until melted. Season to taste with salt and pepper.

3. Return veal chops to pan. Cook for 10 minutes or until desired doneness. Serve veal chops and morel sauce over Parmesan Risotto and Seared Foie Gras.

parmesan **risotto**
makes/4 servings • see photo, page 184

1	tablespoon olive oil
1	onion, diced
1	teaspoon chopped garlic
1	teaspoon chopped shallot
1	cup uncooked Arborio rice
3	cups chicken stock, heated
1	tablespoon chopped fresh thyme
	Salt
	Black pepper
¼	cup grated Parmesan cheese
1	tablespoon unsalted butter

1. In a medium pot heat olive oil over medium heat. Add onion, garlic, and shallot; cook for 3 minutes. Add rice, stirring to coat. Add 1 cup of the hot chicken stock; cook and stir until stock is absorbed.

2. Add another cup of chicken stock; cook and stir until stock is absorbed. Add remaining 1 cup stock; stir in the thyme. Season to taste with salt and pepper. Cook and stir until stock is nearly absorbed. Finish risotto by stirring in the Parmesan cheese and butter.

seared **foie gras**
makes/4 servings • see photo, page 184

¼	cup olive oil
4	ounces foie gras
	Salt
	Black pepper
⅓	cup all-purpose flour

1. In a sauté pan heat olive oil over medium-high heat. (Make sure the pan is heated well.)

2. Season foie gras with salt and pepper. Dredge foie gras in flour to coat. Place foie gras in hot pan and sear for 30 seconds per side or until golden brown.

G's NOTES
For a nice golden crust, make sure the sauté pan is really hot.

whole **prime rib** spiked with garlic and herbs
makes/8 to 10 servings

1   **5-pound whole prime rib**
½   **cup + 3 tablespoons olive oil**
6   **cloves garlic**
2   **tablespoons kosher salt**
2   **tablespoons black pepper**
2   **tablespoons chopped
     fresh thyme**
2   **tablespoons chopped
     fresh rosemary**
2   **tablespoons chopped garlic**
2   **tablespoons chopped shallot**

1. Preheat oven to 350°F. Place prime rib in a roasting pan and coat with ½ cup of the olive oil. Make twelve ½-inch slits on the top of the prime rib. Cut the whole garlic cloves in half and push halves into slits.

2. Season prime rib with salt and pepper, pressing to make sure seasoning sticks. Season with thyme and rosemary. Rub with chopped garlic, shallot, and the remaining 3 tablespoons olive oil.

3. Roast prime rib for 1 ½ hours or until desired doneness. Let stand tented with foil for 15 minutes before carving. Serve with your favorite side dish.

grilled **leg of lamb** with black truffle grits and porcini mushrooms

makes/4 servings

⅓ cup olive oil

3 tablespoons chopped fresh rosemary

3 tablespoons chopped fresh thyme

Kosher salt

Black pepper

4 8-ounce pieces leg of lamb

Black Truffle Grits (see recipe, right)

2 cups canola oil

16 pieces porcini mushrooms

⅔ cup all-purpose flour

1 bunch fresh parsley

Black truffle oil

1. For lamb, in a medium bowl combine olive oil, rosemary, thyme, and salt and pepper to taste. Add lamb and coat well. Refrigerate for 1 hour. Prepare Black Truffle Grits and keep warm.

2. For mushrooms, in a medium saucepan heat canola oil over medium-high heat. Season the mushrooms with salt and pepper to taste. Dredge in flour to coat. Drop mushrooms into the oil and fry for 2 to 3 minutes or until golden. Remove from oil and place on paper towels to absorb excess oil.

3. Grill lamb over medium direct heat for 4 minutes per side or until desired doneness.

4. To serve, place the grits in the middle of the plate. Slice the lamb and fan it out on the grits. Top with the mushrooms and fresh parsley. Drizzle black truffle oil over all.

black truffle grits: In a small saucepan bring 4 cups water and a pinch of salt to a boil. Add 1 cup grits and stir. Add ¼ cup unsalted butter and a pinch of white pepper. Cook and stir over medium heat until grits are thick and creamy white. Fold 1 teaspoon of black truffle oil into the grits.

boneless leg of lamb with smashed potatoes

makes/10 to 12 servings

3	large white onions
½	cup fresh rosemary, chopped
½	cup fresh thyme, chopped
1	cup honey
½	cup + 2 tablespoons olive oil
¼	cup chopped garlic
¼	cup chopped shallot
2	tablespoons salt
1	tablespoon + 1½ teaspoons black pepper
5	pound boneless leg of lamb
8	to 10 medium red potatoes, cut into ½-inch cubes
	Canola oil
1	cup all-purpose flour

1. Cut onions into large chunks and place in a medium bowl. Add rosemary and thyme. Add honey, ½ cup of the olive oil, garlic, shallot, 1 tablespoon of the salt, and 1 tablespoon of the pepper; mix well. Reserve ½ cup herb mixture for potatoes.

2. Pour remaining herb mixture over the leg of lamb; pat mixture into the lamb so herbs will stick. Add a pinch more salt and pepper; set lamb aside.

3. Preheat the oven to 350°F. In a grill pan heat 2 tablespoons olive oil over medium-high heat. Brown lamb on all sides. Transfer lamb to a roasting pan, spooning any herb mixture from pan over lamb. Roast lamb for 1½ hours or until lamb is desired doneness.

4. Meanwhile, for potatoes, in a large pot bring 6 quarts water to a boil. Boil potatoes for 5 to 7 minutes or until cooked. Drain well. With a mallet, lightly smash each potato, leaving them intact. Season with the remaining 1 tablespoon salt and 1½ teaspoons pepper.

5. In a deep fryer or deep frying pan heat enough canola oil to reach halfway up the side of the pan over medium heat. Dredge potatoes in flour, shaking off any excess flour. Cook potatoes in hot oil for 2 to 3 minutes or until golden. Place potatoes on paper towels to absorb excess oil. Toss fried potatoes in a bowl with the reserved herb mixture.

6. To serve, place lamb on a large serving plate and slice into ¼-inch-thick slices. Add potatoes to the serving plate. Drizzle pan juices from roasting pan over lamb.

sautéed **soft-shell crab** and three-cheese polenta
makes/6 servings

4½ cups water
1   cup finely ground polenta
     Salt
¼   cup shredded Gruyère cheese
¼   cup shredded Parmesan cheese
¼   cup goat cheese (chèvre)
¼   cup unsalted butter
     Black pepper
6   large soft-shell crabs
2   teaspoons seasoned salt
1   cup all-purpose flour
½   cup olive oil

1. For polenta, in a large saucepan combine water, polenta, and ½ teaspoon salt. Stir over high heat until mixture boils; reduce heat to medium-low. Simmer polenta for 25 to 30 minutes or until smooth, whisking occasionally to ensure a smooth consistency. Remove from heat and stir in the cheeses and butter; add salt and pepper to taste. Set aside and keep warm.

2. For crab, preheat oven to 375°F. Clean soft-shell crabs by removing the flaps on the undersides and scraping out the gray gill-like material under the shells (pull the top shell back from the side to expose). Sprinkle the crab with seasoned salt, then dredge in flour.

3. In a large ovenproof sauté pan heat olive oil over medium heat. Add crab and sauté on both sides until golden brown. Place pan in the oven for 5 to 7 minutes to finish.

4. To serve, spoon polenta into the center of the plate and top with soft-shell crab.

G's NOTES

Soft-shell crabs are in season from April to mid-September with a peak time in June and July.

Take your time with the polenta. More time and water may be needed. Polenta should not be gritty.

red snapper with **crab gratin**

makes/4 servings

4   **8-ounce boneless, skinless red
       snapper fillets**
     Salt
     Black pepper
     Olive oil
     Crab Gratin (see recipe, right)
     **Maine Lobster Sauce
       (see recipe, opposite)**

1. Preheat oven to 350°F. Season both sides of fillets with salt and pepper. Lightly coat an ovenproof sauté pan with olive oil and heat over medium heat. Fry fillets in pan until golden brown on each side.

2. Place a spoonful of crab gratin mixture on top of each fillet. Sprinkle bread crumb mixture on top of crab gratin and fillets.

3. Bake for 5 to 10 minutes or until bread crumbs are golden brown. Serve with Maine Lobster Sauce.

crab gratin: In a medium bowl stir together 1 pound lump crabmeat, 3 tablespoons Dijon mustard, 3 tablespoons Worcestershire sauce, 2 tablespoons mayonnaise, 2 tablespoons hot sauce, 2 teaspoons chopped fresh parsley, 2 teaspoons Old Bay® seasoning, 1 teaspoon cracked white pepper, and 1 teaspoon black pepper; set aside. In a small bowl mix together 1 cup panko* bread crumbs and 1 tablespoon melted butter; set aside.

* Panko bread crumbs are used in Japanese cooking for coating fried foods. They are coarser than typical dried bread crumbs and make a very crunchy coating.

G's NOTES
Have your fish market remove skin
and bones from snapper fillets.

maine lobster sauce

makes/4 servings

Olive oil
1 **teaspoon chopped garlic**
1 **teaspoon chopped shallot**
4 **ounces cooked lobster, chopped**
4 **ounces lump crabmeat**
3 **ounces cherry tomatoes**
1 **teaspoon salt**
1 **teaspoon black pepper**
1 **cup white wine**
2 **lemons, halved**
1¼ **teaspoons unsalted butter**
1 **teaspoon chopped fresh parsley**

1. Coat a sauté pan with olive oil and heat over medium heat. Add garlic and shallot; stir until lightly browned. Stir in lobster, crabmeat, tomatoes, salt, and pepper.

2. Stir in wine. Squeeze juice from lemons into pan. Stir in butter and parsley. Simmer for 3 minutes or until sauce starts to thicken.

mussels with white wine sauce and basil mayonnaise

makes/4 servings

¼ cup olive oil
1 tablespoon chopped garlic
1 tablespoon chopped shallot
1 pound mussels, cleaned
½ cup white wine
3 tablespoons butter, melted
   Kosher salt
   Cracked black pepper
2 jalapeño peppers, sliced
     (see tip, page 207)
   Basil Mayonnaise
     (see recipe, right)

1. Preheat oven to 375°F. In a large oven-safe sauté pan heat olive oil over medium heat. Add garlic and shallot; sauté for 1 minute. Add mussels and white wine; cook until mussels open.

2. Drizzle mussels with melted butter and a pinch each of salt and black pepper. Sprinkle jalapeño slices over top. Place in oven until most of the liquid has evaporated from the mussels..

3. To serve, place mussels on a platter and spoon Basil Mayonnaise over top.

basil mayonnaise: In a food processor combine 1 cup mayonnaise, 5 tablespoons chopped fresh basil, 1 tablespoon chopped garlic, 1 tablespoon chopped shallot, and 1 tablespoon lemon juice. Pulse until smooth.

G's NOTES
You can mix basil mayonnaise in a bowl with a whisk, if you desire.

maine lobster mashed potatoes with wasabi

makes/4 servings

6   white rose potatoes, peeled and quartered
1   1¼-pound lobster
3   tablespoons olive oil
   Kosher salt
   Black pepper
2   tablespoons unsalted butter
1   tablespoon chopped garlic
1   cup heavy cream
2   tablespoons water
1   tablespoon wasabi powder

1. Place a large pot of water and a smaller pot of water on the stove; bring both to a boil. Place potatoes in the larger pot and boil until tender; drain and set aside.

2. Crack the claws of the lobster and place it in the second pot of boiling water; boil for 5 minutes. Remove lobster from pot and place in a bowl or sink of ice water. Drain and pat dry. Split lobster down the middle. In a bowl combine the olive oil and a pinch of salt and pepper. Add lobster, turning to coat well; set aside.

3. Remove lobster from bowl, draining excess oil. Grill over medium direct heat for 3 to 5 minutes or until shell is slightly charred. Set aside to cool. Remove shell and rough cut the lobster meat. Set aside.

4. In a medium saucepan melt butter over medium heat. Add garlic; sauté until tender. Add cream and bring to a simmer. Mash the cooked potatoes. Slowly whip hot cream mixture into the potatoes until desired consistency. Season to taste with salt and pepper. In a small bowl mix together the water and wasabi powder until smooth; stir into mashed potatoes. Fold lobster into mashed potatoes.

seafood pasta with a creamy **white wine sauce**
makes/4 to 6 servings

10	tablespoons olive oil
	Salt
	Black pepper
7	medium mussels
6	medium clams
6	sea scallops
8	medium shrimp
2	king crab legs, cut into 2-inch pieces
1	pound linguine
2	tablespoons butter
2	tablespoons chopped garlic
2	tablespoons chopped shallot
½	cup white wine
¼	cup heavy cream
4	whole basil leaves
2	tablespoons grated parmesan cheese

1. In a stockpot bring 2 quarts water to a boil. Add 4 tablespoons of the olive oil, a pinch of salt, and a pinch of pepper.

2. Place seafood in a baking pan and coat with 2 tablespoons of the olive oil. Season seafood with salt and pepper.

3. In a grill pan heat 2 tablespoons of the olive oil over medium heat. Place mussels and clams in the pan; cook for 1 to 2 minutes or until shells begin to open. Add the scallops, shrimp, and crab legs; cook for 3 to 4 minutes or until scallops, shrimp, and crab are opaque. Set aside.

4. Meanwhile, add the linguine to the boiling water. Cook for 6 to 7 minutes or until tender but firm. Drain and set aside.

5. In a large frying pan heat the remaining 2 tablespoons olive oil and the butter over medium heat. Add the garlic and shallot; sauté for 1 minute. Add the white wine. Slowly add the cream and mix well. Add the basil, parmesan cheese, and a pinch of salt and pepper; mix well.

6. Add cooked linguine to the cream sauce and mix well. Add all the seafood to the pan and mix well. Pour linguine and seafood into a large serving bowl. Season to taste with additional salt and pepper.

three-cheese vegetable lasagna with cream sauce
makes/12 servings

1 **16-ounce package lasagna noodles**
1 **small head broccoli, sliced to lie flat**
1 **small head cauliflower, sliced to lie flat**
  Salt
  Black pepper
2 **cups shredded carrot**
1 **cup ricotta cheese**
3½ **cups heavy cream**
4 **tablespoons unsalted butter**
3 **tablespoons chopped garlic**
3 **tablespoons chopped shallot**
1¾ **cups shredded Parmesan cheese**
¾ **cup chicken stock**
4 **ounces baby spinach, sliced**
1 **pound mozzarella cheese, shredded**

1. Preheat oven to 425°F. Cook noodles as directed on package. Drain; set aside.

2. In a pot of boiling water boil broccoli and cauliflower for 5 minutes. Remove from pot and place in a bowl of ice water. Drain and pat dry. Place broccoli and cauliflower in a large bowl and toss with salt and pepper to taste. Spread in an even layer on an ungreased baking sheet.

3. In the same bowl place the shredded carrot; toss with salt and pepper to taste. Spread carrot out on a separate ungreased baking sheet. Place both sheets in the oven and roast for 7 to 10 minutes or until vegetables are lightly browned. Remove from oven and set aside.

4. Reduce oven temperature to 350°F. In a separate bowl combine ricotta cheese, ¼ cup of the cream, and a pinch each of salt and pepper. Set aside.

5. In a large saucepan melt 2 tablespoons of the butter over medium heat. Add garlic and shallot; sauté for 1 to 2 minutes or until tender but not brown. Add the remaining 3¼ cups cream to the pan. (Do not boil.) Slowly stir in 1¼ cups of the Parmesan cheese and the chicken stock. Stir with a whisk until smooth and creamy. Remove sauce from heat.

6. Spread a little sauce over the bottom of a 13×9×2-inch baking pan. Arrange 3 or 4 noodles over sauce in bottom of pan. Using a rubber spatula, spread ricotta cheese over noodles. Top with a layer of spinach followed by half of the roasted vegetables. Sprinkle one-third of the mozzarella cheese over vegetables and sprinkle a little Parmesan over top.

7. Repeat layers until all is used. Sprinkle the last of the Parmesan cheese over the top and add the rest of the sauce. Bake, uncovered, for 30 to 40 minutes or until hot and mozzarella cheese is light brown.

chapter eight

sweet
thoughts

{ End your meal happily with tempting
desserts. One bite is just not enough! }

A great dessert, like life, takes a little patience. Sure, you can throw things together for some recipes, but a great-tasting dessert requires care and planning. At the end of a long day, you might not want to put the extra time into fixing dessert, but trust me, the results are worth the effort. When the dinner silverware is dirty and the linens are stained and they've all cleaned their plates, bringing out a great dessert gives you a chance to really enjoy the end of a meal—just like everything else in the kitchen—super simple. In the end, I think you'll see that dessert is truly what life is all about—good times, good food, keeping it real, and keeping it smooth.

mixed berry delight

makes/6 to 8 servings • see photo, page 189

2 cups heavy cream
3 tablespoons powdered sugar
1 teaspoon vanilla extract
2 tablespoons water
2 tablespoons granulated sugar
1 cup fresh blackberries
1 cup fresh blueberries
1 cup fresh golden raspberries
1 cup fresh red raspberries
1 cup sliced fresh strawberries
1 star fruit, peeled and sliced
1 bunch fresh mint leaves
¼ cup chocolate sauce

1. Place a metal bowl in the freezer and let chill about 20 minutes. Place cream in chilled bowl and beat with a whisk until soft peaks form. Add powdered sugar and vanilla and continue to whisk until stiff peaks form. Set whipped cream aside.

2. In a small saucepan combine water and granulated sugar. Heat over medium heat until sugar is dissolved. Set simple syrup aside.

3. In a large bowl place all berries and star fruit; gently mix together. Add simple syrup. Chop about 3 mint leaves and add to bowl; gently mix. Drizzle with chocolate sauce. Top with whipped cream.

G'S NOTES

This great dessert can be served family-style by placing whipped cream on top, or it can be spooned into martini glasses and drizzled with chocolate sauce for that stepped-up approach. It also could be served over a scoop of ice cream. Use just one or all of your favorite berries to personalize it.

trifle cake

makes/12 to 16 servings • see photo, page 190

1   24-ounce jar strawberry jam
2   16-ounce loaves pound cake,
       sliced
4   cups vanilla pudding*
2   cups heavy cream, whipped
2   pints fresh strawberries, sliced
¼   cup sliced or slivered almonds,
       toasted
½   cup chocolate syrup

1. In a sauté pan heat strawberry jam until it has reached a smooth consistency. Set aside.

2. In the bottom of a large glass bowl place a layer of pound cake slices. Spread some jam over the cake. Continue by adding a layer of pudding on top of the jam, then add a layer of whipped cream. Top whipped cream with a layer of sliced strawberries.

3. Repeat layers until dessert is desired height. Top with toasted almonds and drizzle with chocolate syrup.

* If you like, make your favorite pudding recipe for this one.

 's NOTES

I like to serve this in a clear glass trifle bowl to show off the very colorful layers. Inquire at your local housewares store for a trifle bowl.

7-up® cake

makes/12 servings

3 cups sugar
1½ cups (3 sticks) butter, softened
5 eggs
3¼ cups all-purpose flour
¾ cup 7-UP
1 tablespoon lemon extract
1 tablespoon vanilla extract
½ cup plain yogurt

1. Make sure all ingredients are at room temperature. Preheat oven to 350°F.

2. In a large mixing bowl cream together sugar and butter. Beat in eggs, one at a time. Mix in flour and 7-UP, ¼ cup at a time, until well blended. Stir in lemon extract and vanilla. Fold in yogurt. Turn batter into a greased and floured 10-inch fluted tube pan or a 9×5 inch loaf pan.

3. Bake for 45 minutes or until golden brown and a toothpick inserted in the middle of the cake comes out clean.

fresh **peaches and raspberries**
in grand marnier® sauce over pound cake

makes/6 servings

¼ cup Grand Marnier
     (orange-flavored liqueur)
2   tablespoons honey
1   tablespoon packed light
     brown sugar
9   mint leaves (3 chopped
     and 6 for garnish)
1   teaspoon orange zest
2   fresh peaches, peeled,
     pitted, and sliced
1   pint raspberries
1   pound cake (purchased
     or see recipe, below)
     Whipped cream

1. In a bowl combine Grand Marnier, honey, brown sugar, chopped mint, and the orange zest; mix well. Add peaches and raspberries. Toss lightly; set aside for 20 minutes.

2. Slice pound cake. Spoon fruit mixture over pound cake slices. Garnish with whipped cream and whole mint leaves.

pound **cake**

makes/10 to 12 servings

2   cups cake flour
1   tablespoon baking powder
½ teaspoon baking soda
¼ teaspoon salt
1   pound butter, softened
1   cup granulated sugar
1   cup packed brown sugar
5   large eggs
3   tablespoons sour cream
2   teaspoons vanilla extract
1   teaspoon lemon extract

1. Preheat oven to 325°F. Sift the flour, baking powder, baking soda, and salt together into a large bowl; set aside.

2. In a separate mixing bowl mix together the butter, granulated sugar, and brown sugar with a whisk or electric mixer until creamed. Beat in eggs, one at a time, mixing well after each addition. Whisk in sour cream, then the vanilla and lemon extract. Add flour mixture, folding to combine thoroughly.

3. Turn batter into a greased 9×5-inch loaf pan. Bake for 1 hour or until golden brown and a toothpick inserted into the center comes out clean.

 's NOTES
Make sure all ingredients are at room temperature.

chocolate **bread pudding**

makes/12 servings

2 tablespoons unsalted butter

1½ loaves French or Portuguese bread, cubed

1 cup coarsely chopped pecans, walnuts, or almonds

¼ cup semisweet chocolate pieces

¼ cup white chocolate pieces

¼ cup milk chocolate pieces

5 eggs

2 cups milk

1 cup sugar

¾ cup white corn syrup

¼ cup rum

1 tablespoon vanilla extract
   Whipped cream (optional)

1. Preheat oven to 350°F. Use butter to grease a 13×9×2-inch baking dish. Place dry bread cubes in the bottom dish. Sprinkle the nuts and all the chocolate pieces over bread cubes; set aside.

2. In a large bowl beat together eggs, milk, sugar, corn syrup, rum, and vanilla. Pour egg mixture over the bread mixture. Gently push down on the bread cubes with the back of a large spoon, making sure the bread absorbs the egg mixture and the chocolate pieces and nuts are covered with the egg mixture.

3. Bake for 50 to 60 minutes or until a knife inserted near the center comes out clean. If the top starts to overbrown, cover loosely with foil until custard is set. Remove from oven and let cool. If desired, top each serving with whipped cream.

rice pudding

makes/12 servings

¼ cup raisins
¼ cup water
2 tablespoons vanilla extract
1 Red Delicious apple,
    peeled and diced
2 tablespoons unsalted butter
1 teaspoon ground cinnamon
1 teaspoon ground nutmeg
3 large egg yolks
¾ cup sugar
1 cup milk
3 cups cooked rice
  Crushed Oreo® cookies
  Chocolate sauce
  Crushed walnuts
  Caramel sauce
  Whipped cream

1. Preheat oven to 300°F. Soak raisins in the ¼ cup water and 1 tablespoon of the vanilla for 20 minutes. In a sauté pan cook apple in butter with cinnamon and nutmeg over medium heat until tender. Set aside.

2. Meanwhile, bring a medium pot of water to a boil. Place egg yolks in a medium bowl. Place bowl with egg yolks over boiling water. (Note: This creates a hot water bath.) Use a whisk to stir yolks at a steady rate. Remove bowl periodically from pot so eggs don't scramble and return bowl to hot water bath just enough to heat eggs. When eggs are hot, add the sugar and whisk briskly.

3. In a separate pan heat milk over low heat until steaming. Once milk is hot, whisk it into eggs and sugar. Whisk in the remaining 1 tablespoon vanilla.

4. Place rice in a 13×9×2-inch baking dish. Drain the raisins, pressing out any excess liquid. Add raisins and sautéed apples to rice. Spread mixture in dish. Pour the hot milk mixture over the rice. Stir to combine.

5. Bake for 25 to 30 minutes or until set. Remove from oven and let stand for 10 minutes; chill.

6. In a small dessert bowl or martini glass place a small amount of crushed Oreos. Drizzle with chocolate sauce. Top with a spoonful of rice pudding. Sprinkle walnuts over pudding and drizzle with caramel sauce. Top with more pudding and chocolate sauce. Finish with whipped cream. Repeat for remaining servings.

 G's NOTES

The consistency of the pudding should be moist but not loose.

sweet potato pie

makes/2 pies (12 to 16 servings) • see photo, page 191

6   sweet potatoes
½   cup sugar
4   large eggs
½   cup sweetened condensed milk
½   cup heavy cream
¼   cup unsalted butter, softened
1   tablespoon vanilla extract
2   teaspoons ground cinnamon
2   9-inch pie shells (see Pastry
    For Two Single-Crust Pies
    recipe, below)

1. Preheat oven to 350°F. Bake whole potatoes for 1 hour or until soft. When potatoes are cool enough to handle, peel and mash them in a large bowl. Add sugar, eggs, sweetened condensed milk, cream, butter, vanilla, and cinnamon; mix well.

2. Prebake pie shells in the 350°F oven for 2 to 3 minutes or until lightly browned. Remove from oven and pour sweet potato mixture evenly into shells. Bake for 35 minutes more or until firm.

pastry for two single-crust pies

makes/2 crusts

2½   cups flour
3   tablespoons sugar
1   teaspoon salt
1   cup (2 sticks) butter, cubed
1   egg
¼   cup cold water

1. In a mixing bowl stir together flour, sugar, and salt. Using a fork, cut in butter until pieces are pea size. Mix egg and water together; sprinkle some of the mixture over flour mixture. Gently toss with fork. Repeat moistening flour mixture until all the flour mixture is moistened. Form pastry into a ball; divide in half.

2. On a lightly floured surface use your hands to slightly flatten one portion of pastry. Roll into a circle 12 inches in diameter. Ease into pie plate; prick bottom and sides with a fork. Repeat with remaining pastry.

G's NOTES

To blind bake, place a sheet of parchment paper into the center of the dough that is in the pie form and spread it out to the sides. Then carefully pour in raw beans, any type—lima, pinto, or field peas and bake for 5 to 7 minutes or until slightly golden.

sweet potato mousse

makes/6 to 8 servings

1 large sweet potato
¼ cup packed brown sugar
¼ teaspoon ground ginger
¼ teaspoon ground cinnamon
¼ teaspoon vanilla extract
1¼ cups heavy cream
1 package unflavored gelatin
3 egg whites
1 teaspoon fresh lemon juice
½ cup powdered sugar
 Coconut, toasted (optional)

1. Preheat oven to 375°F. Bake sweet potato for 30 to 40 minutes or until soft. When potato is cool enough to handle, peel off skin. Place potato in the bowl of an electric mixer. Add brown sugar. Using the wire whip attachment, beat with electric mixer until smooth, removing any strings that collect on the whip. Add ginger, cinnamon, and vanilla; mix well. Using a rubber spatula, press sweet potato mixture through a hand strainer to remove all lumps. Set aside.

2. In a small saucepan combine ¼ cup of the cream and the gelatin. Heat over low heat until gelatin is dissolved, stirring constantly. Add to sweet potato mixture; mix well. Chill sweet potato mixture until set.

3. In a bowl beat egg whites and lemon juice with an electric mixer until soft peaks start to form. Add ¼ cup of the powdered sugar and beat on high speed until egg whites are bright white and stiff. Set aside.

4. Beat the remaining 1 cup cream and ¼ cup powdered sugar until stiff peak forms. Fold half of the whipped cream into chilled sweet potato mixture. Gently fold beaten egg whites into sweet potato mixture. Chill.

5. To serve, pipe or spoon sweet potato mousse into your favorite dish or dishes. Top with remaining whipped cream and, if desired, toasted coconut.

banana cream pie

makes/6 to 8 servings

1   box graham crackers
½   cup finely chopped pecans
⅔   cup packed brown sugar
¾   cup (1½ sticks) butter, melted
3¼ cups milk
6   egg yolks
1⅓ cups granulated sugar
½   cup unbleached flour
⅓   cup cornstarch
2   ripe bananas, peeled and sliced
½   teaspoon vanilla extract

1. Preheat oven to 375°F. For crust, place graham crackers and pecans in a food processor; pulse until fine. Add brown sugar and melted butter; pulse until combined well. Pour mixture into a pie plate; press firmly into bottom and up sides of plate. Bake for 10 to 15 minutes or until browned. Remove crust from oven and set aside.

2. For filling, in a saucepan heat 3 cups of the milk over medium heat until steaming. In a bowl whisk together the remaining ¼ cup milk, the egg yolks, granulated sugar, flour, and cornstarch. Slowly whisk 1 cup of the hot milk into the egg mixture. Pour warm egg mixture into saucepan with hot milk. Cook and stir until mixture thickens and starts to bubble. Remove custard from heat; set aside.

3. In the food processor place sliced bananas and the vanilla. Pour custard over bananas and pulse until smooth. Pour filling into baked crust. Chill for 4 hours or until set.

banana fritters

makes/8 servings

¾ cup sifted all-purpose flour
2 tablespoons granulated sugar
  Pinch salt
2 eggs
2 tablespoons water
2 tablespoons milk
⅛ teaspoon grated lemon zest
  Pinch ground nutmeg
  Peanut oil
4 large firm, ripe bananas
3 tablespoons powdered sugar

1. In a medium bowl stir together the flour, granulated sugar, and salt; make a well in the center. Separate the eggs;* set whites aside. Place egg yolks in the well in the flour mixture. Mix the egg yolks into the flour mixture, gradually mixing in the water and milk. Set batter aside.

2. In a second bowl beat egg whites with an electric mixer on high speed until stiff peaks form. Gently fold whites into batter. Stir in lemon zest and nutmeg. Cover the bowl of batter with a clean, damp towel and place it in the refrigerator for the day.

3. When ready to prepare fritters, in a heavy Dutch oven or deep fryer heat 2 inches of peanut oil to 375°F.

4. Peel the bananas and cut them crosswise into 1-inch pieces. With tongs, dip the pieces into the batter, then fry them in the hot oil until they are golden brown on each side. With a slotted spoon, remove fritters from oil and let them drain on paper towels to remove excess oil.

5. Place fritters on a serving plate. Place the powdered sugar in a fine-mesh sieve and shake it over the fritters. Serve warm.

* When separating the eggs, be careful not to get any egg yolk into the whites. Even a little yolk can keep the whites from beating to stiff peaks.

G's NOTES
These fritters may also be served with whipped cream, chocolate sauce, strawberries, and fresh mint or any of your favorite toppings.

peach **cobbler**

makes/12 servings

- 4 cups all-purpose flour
- 4 teaspoons baking powder
- 1 teaspoon granulated sugar
- ½ teaspoon salt
- 1 cup vegetable shortening
- ⅔ cup buttermilk
  Nonstick cooking spray
- 3 16-ounce cans sliced peaches
- 2 cups granulated sugar
- 2 tablespoons packed brown sugar
- 2 tablespoons unsalted butter
- 2 teaspoons ground cinnamon
- 1 teaspoon ground nutmeg
- 2 teaspoons vanilla extract
- 2 tablespoons cornstarch
- 4 teaspoons water
- 1 teaspoon lemon juice
- 1 egg
- 1 tablespoon water
- 1 teaspoon granulated sugar

1. Preheat oven to 350°F. In a bowl sift together the flour, baking powder, 1 teaspoon granulated sugar, and the salt. Using a fork, work in the shortening until mixture resembles coarse crumbs. Slowly add buttermilk to flour mixture, blending until incorporated. Work with hands to form dough into a ball.

2. Cut dough ball in half. On a lightly floured surface roll out one half into a 14×12-inch rectangle. Spray a 13×9×2-inch baking dish with nonstick cooking spray. Place dough in baking dish, halfway up the sides. Prick entire bottom and sides of dough with a fork. Bake for 4 minutes or until golden. Set shell aside.

3. Drain peaches; reserve liquid. Place peaches in a pot; add 2 cups of the reserved liquid. Add the 2 cups granulated sugar, the brown sugar, butter, cinnamon, nutmeg, and vanilla. Cook on medium heat for 5 to 6 minutes. In a glass measure, mix together cornstarch, water, and lemon juice; add to peach mixture. Cook over low heat for 4 minutes more. Remove from heat. Pour mixture into baked shell.

4. Roll out the second half of the dough and cover the top of the filling. Randomly make about 6 to 7 slashes into the dough about ½ inch long. Mix together egg and water to make an egg wash. With a pastry brush, brush egg wash over top of crust. Sprinkle 1 teaspoon granulated sugar over crust. Place in oven and bake for 30 to 45 minutes or until crust is golden.

 G's NOTES

Your dough may not roll out to form a perfect rectangle. Try to get as close as you can and trim off the edges where necessary. Before placing the dough on top, fold it in half carefully. Lay it on top of the peaches, then unfold the dough and seal the edges.

touchdown **brownies**

makes/12 servings

1   cup (2 sticks) unsalted butter
4   1-ounce squares unsweetened
    chocolate
2   cups sugar
1   cup all-purpose flour
4   eggs
1   cup crushed pecans, walnuts,
    and almonds
2   teaspoons vanilla extract
    Butter

toppings:
Hershey's® chocolate bar pieces
Crushed and whole M&M's®
Crushed Oreo® cookies
Snickers® candy bar pieces
Caramel sauce
Chocolate sauce
Whipped cream
Crushed nuts
Multicolored sprinkles
Mint leaves

1. Preheat oven to 350°F. Bring a pot of water to a boil and place a metal bowl or double boiler over it. Add butter and chocolate squares to bowl over water and stir until melted. Pour melted chocolate mixture into a large glass bowl. Add sugar, flour, eggs, nuts, and vanilla; mix well.

2. Line a 13×9×2-inch baking dish with parchment paper. Rub parchment paper with butter to prevent sticking, then pour brownie batter into dish. Bake about 30 minutes or until a wooden toothpick inserted in the center comes out clean. Remove brownies from oven and let cool.

3. Use parchment paper to lift brownies from baking dish. Cut into bars. Top brownies as desired with toppings.

oreo® cheesecake squares

makes/12 servings

3 cups Oreo cookie crumbs
9 tablespoons butter, melted
⅓ cup cold water
1 package unflavored gelatin
12 ounces cream cheese, softened
¾ cup sugar
1¼ cups milk
1½ cups heavy cream
¼ cup powdered sugar
20 Oreo cookies, chopped

1. Preheat oven to 350°F. For crust, in a bowl combine cookie crumbs and melted butter; mix well. Press mixture into bottom and 1½ inches up the sides of a 13×9×2-inch baking pan. Bake crust for 10 minutes; set aside.

2. For filling, place water in a saucepan. Stir gelatin into water. Heat and stir over low heat until dissolved; set aside. In a medium bowl combine cream cheese and sugar until well blended. Stir in gelatin and milk until blended. Chill until thickened but not set.

3. In a large bowl beat the cream and powdered sugar until stiff peaks form. Fold whipped cream into cream cheese mixture. Pour half of the filling into baked crust. Top with half of the chopped cookies. Top with remaining filling and then with remaining chopped cookies. Chill until firm. Cut into squares to serve.

 's NOTES

After the cookies and butter are mixed for the crust, placing the mixture in the refrigerator to chill first makes it easier to pack the crust into the baking dish.

final thoughts

I'm not a famous doctor, scientist, or civil rights leader. I am a guy who cooks. My responsibility is to make lives better through food. It is not brain surgery.

What counts is hanging out with a bunch of people you care about over a meal. And it doesn't always have to be a stellar meal. I've screwed up a dish or two myself, but I stay with it because I care.

Whatever you do, know that it is important to people. They may not tell you, but it is. So find that thing that you love and share it. You never know what a difference it might make in the life of someone else.

And at the end of the day, remember that this is God's planet and we are all just visitors. It is our responsibility to take care of each other while we are here. Let's get back to the days of sharing, caring, door holding, chair pulling, and good old-fashioned common courtesy. I promise we'll all have a better place to call home. And at your next dinner, do as a couple of my dearest friends D.L. and LaDonna Hughley have retaught me: Hold hands, say a prayer, and bless the food, family, and friends.

index

Food photographs are noted in green numerals.

index

Food photographs are noted in green numerals.

index

index

see what we see

Lifestyle & Entertainment Television

Available on Direct TV Channel 241
Check CABLE LISTINGS in your area

For more about G. Garvin go to
www.tvoneonline.com